Praise for *The Miseducation of the Student Athlete*

Winner of 2018 Axiom Business Book Award Bronze Medal

Winner of 2018 eLit Book Award Gold Medal

"When grades take a back seat to the playing field, the term 'student athlete' can appear to be contradictory. Shropshire (Global Sport/ Arizona State; *Sport Matters*, 2015, etc.) and debut author Williams seek to change this perception, arguing that, while athletics pay off for a select few, education benefits almost everyone . . . . As academics, the authors are used to marshaling evidence to support their assertions, and the research they lay out here is impressive. It's clear that they're no fans of the present system, yet their discussion is refreshingly free of displays of cynicism and outrage. An uncompromising look at America's college-sports conundrum, offering a controversial solution that just might work."
—***Kirkus Reviews***

"Kenneth L. Shropshire and Collin D. Williams, Jr., examine a controversial issue that many choose to ignore because it is either uncomfortable or not financially beneficial for them to do so. I applaud Shropshire and Williams for providing an in-depth analysis of the present reality called life for student-athletes. The public needs to analyze who benefits the most, in the long-term, from student participation in intercollegiate athletics. This is a must-read for anyone truly interested in participating in the conversation."
—**Brandon Copeland, Defensive End, Detroit Lions, National Football League**

THE MISEDUCATION OF THE STUDENT ATHLETE

HOW TO FIX COLLEGE SPORTS

KENNETH L. SHROPSHIRE
COLLIN D. WILLIAMS, JR.

WHARTON
SCHOOL
PRESS
Philadelphia

Published by Wharton School Press
The Wharton School
University of Pennsylvania
3620 Locust Walk
2000 Steinberg Hall-Dietrich Hall
Philadelphia, PA 19104
Email: whartonschoolpress@wharton.upenn.edu
Website: http://wsp.wharton.upenn.edu

Ebook ISBN: 978-1-61363-081-5
Paperback ISBN: 978-1-61363-082-2

9 8 7 6 5 4 3 2

Contents

Foreword

They come as 17- and 18-year-old recent high school graduates. In the two sports that generate the largest sums of money (men's basketball and football), they are overwhelmingly Black and poor; their coaches are mostly white and outrageously well compensated. Because of punitive National Collegiate Athletic Association (NCAA) policies, they are not allowed to have agents negotiate the terms of their engagement and relationships with multimillion-dollar enterprises to which they commit to live, learn, and work. Few have people to fully and honestly explain to them the extent to which they will labor.

So many are first in their families to attend college. They do not know what questions to ask when coaches seduce them and their parents with what sounds like life-changing opportunities and sure pathways to the National Football League (NFL), National Basketball Association (NBA), and other major league professional sports organizations after college. Because of this, they start their freshman year thinking they have full scholarships, four years of guaranteed financial support; they do not understand that coaches determine whether their scholarships are renewed from one year to the next, or what happens if they get injured and can no longer play. Too little information is given to them about academics, campus life outside of athletics, and the importance of participating in enriching educational experiences (for example, study abroad, internships in their fields, and collaborative research projects with faculty members). They are teenagers who do not know enough about exploitation— they just want to play the sport they love while taking advantage of a "free" college scholarship. By the time they realize they have been manipulated, it is too late.

Many colleges and universities take advantage of the limited information that prospective students and their families have about the business of intercollegiate athletics. This phenomenon is recurrent, inescapably racialized, and gendered in particular ways. This is wrong and especially injurious to young Black men who earn billions for their universities, athletic conferences, and the NCAA, a so-called nonprofit. On average, football coaches in Power 5 conferences earn annual salaries of $3.26 million; head coaches of men's basketball teams earn $2.88 million. Black men are only 16.2% of these head coaches. Also, the five conference commissioners earn, on average, annual salaries of $2.58 million. Each is a white man. College students (specifically, Black undergraduate men), for the most part, pay these men's salaries.

No one can reasonably argue that what student-athletes receive is a fair share of what they earn. They do not. The challenge, though, is that institutions of higher education are supposed to be hallmarks of enlightenment and learning, not professional sports organizations. But the reality is that too many athletics departments are driven by ticket sales, television contracts, alumni donations, and winning seasons that protect coaches from termination. This often occurs at the expense of academic success, personal development, and the accumulation of professional skills and experiences that poise student-athletes to compete successfully for meaningful careers and admission to top graduate schools.

As Kenneth Shropshire and Collin Williams masterfully document in this important book, universities effectively miseducate student-athletes. Though a lover of intercollegiate sports, I am one of the harshest critics of the role universities play in exploiting mostly Black male teams of revenue generators. To be sure, I would still care if there were fewer Black men on fields and courts. I believe universities should not be in the business of exploiting any person, let alone teenagers who know very little about the economics of the enterprise. Shropshire and Williams have written a helpful, consciousness-raising book that will hopefully compel student-athletes and those who care about them to demand more appropriate remuneration for the labor from which universities, conferences, and the NCAA profit.

Shaun R. Harper, PhD
University of Southern California
Marshall School of Business and
Rossier School of Education

Preface

Can we fix college sports? That broad but daunting question sparked a conversation between the two of us that ultimately led to this book and our overarching argument.

Kenneth Shropshire was finishing a career at the University of Pennsylvania's Wharton School. This topic had been one of many he contemplated during a career focused on how sport can make the people associated with it, and the world, better. Having just accepted an offer to serve as the CEO of the new Global Sport Institute at Arizona State University, he was preparing to investigate these issues even more deeply. Around the same time, an eye-opening experience revealed how much college sport had changed since his days as a scholarship student-athlete on the Stanford University football team.

Ken watched his son, Sam Shropshire, strive to excel as both a student and an athlete as one of the leaders of the tennis team at Northwestern University. "Doing both"—being both student *and* athlete—was a very different proposition than it had been in the 1970s. Four decades ago at Stanford and elsewhere, the stories of those playing at the varsity level while also pursuing a premed, engineering, or some other rigorous degree program were not uncommon. Today, however, student-athletes excelling in both athletics and academics seem to be much more scarce. The mindset that exists within every major sports program is that any time you are not practicing or preparing for competition, you are preparing to lose. So rather than focusing on their academic studies, student-athletes are regularly in the gym or weight room, or studying film of their plays and future opponents. Simply put, sports come first. Academics is a distant second.

As closely as Ken had studied sport through the years, he found through watching his son that his perception of what student-athletes endure was antiquated. Though Sam graduated on time, with a meaningful degree in hand and the opportunity to play professionally, Ken realized academic and athletic success was, sadly, no longer the norm. Rather, the women and men who achieved both in four or five years were, in a word, exceptional.

Adding to Ken's wake-up call was the dissertation written by Collin Williams. Collin had just completed his doctorate in higher education at the University of Pennsylvania's Graduate School of Education after defending a dissertation examining how high-profile athletes made sense of their college experience. Filled with interviews on this very topic, Collin's study used student-athletes' own words to explain what they endured. The 40 college football players from 28 colleges and universities across each of the Power 5 conferences shared enlightening narratives that made clear that time, or the lack thereof, is the main barrier to academic and professional success for the modern student-athlete. At the elite levels, it has become increasingly impossible to balance school and sports, much less a social life or other extracurricular activities. Both authors felt these rarely heard voices needed to reach a wider readership. The experiences and insights student-athletes shared with Collin are featured throughout.

In *The Miseducation of the Student Athlete*, we present our thoughts on what must be done to transform college sports and improve the student-athlete experience. We argue that in the world of collegiate athletics, while sport pays off for a select few, education can pay off for most. At a minimum, we aim to open a gateway for broader thinking by policymakers and activists on how to increase the likelihood of student-athletes succeeding both on and off the field. The discussion is particularly timely, as staggering media rights deals are pouring tons of new revenues into college sports. Understandably, this has led to a surge in public discourse on whether participants should be paid. We intervene seeking to redirect the conversation away from paying student-athletes and to first better *educating* them. For reasons detailed later, we contend education is the best compensation.

We focus significant attention on the leaders of college sport, often wrongly perceived to be just the National Collegiate Athletic Association (NCAA). Though the Indianapolis-based association may appear to be some monolith operating as an enterprise, the NCAA is, in fact, an association of member institutions. Thus, numerous stakeholders at the conference and institutional levels also bear the responsibility of change. This includes the athletes themselves. In the final chapter, we use the Sports Power Matrix—which Ken first introduced in his book *Sport Matters*—to sort through the various parties and powers involved in the college sports enterprise.

The inspiration for the book's title comes from Carter G. Woodson's *The Mis-education of the Negro*. Known as "the father of Black history," Woodson earned a doctorate from Harvard in 1912, becoming the second African-American to do so (W. E. B. DuBois was the first). In his landmark work, he encouraged African-Americans to demand educational opportunities relevant to their culture and experiences. This is notable because, while the broad concept of miseducation is applicable to anyone, the nature of this problem is crucially important for Black men, the largest demographic in revenue-generating college sports. Though the reforms we propose are aimed at improving conditions for all, this particular segment may stand to benefit most. If college sports are to be fixed, these student-athletes must overcome what Woodson refers to as "back door" thinking.

> If you can control a man's thinking you do not have to worry about his action. When you determine what a man shall think you do not have to concern yourself about what he will do. If you make a man feel that he is inferior, you do not have to compel him to accept an inferior status, for he will seek it himself. If you make a man think that he is justly an outcast, you do not

have to order him to the back door. He will go without being told; and if there is no back door, his very nature will demand one.[1]

As they begin college, students playing high-profile sports are forced to choose between school (the front door) and the lucrative careers that may come with sports (the back door). Sold the dream that sports are the best chance at a better life, they regularly choose the back door, trying to beat the odds and make it professionally. Laser focused on athletic success, elite student-athletes make academic sacrifices they often later regret. Recognizing this way of thinking is normative among some student-athlete populations, we strive to create a system where a variety of paths to academic success lie behind whichever door an athlete initially chooses.

What follows is our vision on how to get student-athletes to take advantage of the once-in-a-lifetime educational opportunity that a scholarship should present. We firmly believe it is time to rethink how we have been educating student-athletes and what they are expected to accomplish in the traditional time frame. The goal is to help as many student-athletes as possible earn meaningful degrees and establish fulfilling careers.

Introduction
Righting a Misguided Discourse

I've had so many teammates say to me, "Aye, man. I'm really dis-
appointed. I can't believe I'm graduating with this degree and
don't have any jobs lined up. I wish I had done something more
along the lines of what you're doing, like accounting or something like that." Guys aren't really given the time, resources, and
sometimes, the option, to think about what would be most valuable in terms of a degree. If the big payoff of being in college is
making the most of that degree and getting lifelong benefits out
of it, the greatest cost of playing football and basketball at this
level is that you have to consider changing what it is you want to
study. Unless you make it to the NFL or NBA, the easy under-
grad degree doesn't really give you much earning potential.[2]

By the time he was a second-semester senior, John[3] had already
played four years of football for a highly competitive program,
networked with alums to land several job shadows, and secured
full-time employment after graduation. Speaking somewhat abash-
edly about his success, he explained that this was not the case for
most of his teammates. While many would be donning their caps
and gowns in a couple of months, few knew what they would be
doing after they received their degrees, much less what they were
good at, or even interested in, besides football. When asked what
led to the stark differences between him and his peers, John spoke of

his upbringing and how it impacted his orientation to football and school. For starters, he was a walk-on that made the team via tryouts, which means he was admitted to college on the basis of his grades rather than his football talent. Additionally, coming from a middle-class family, John did not view sports as "the way out." For sure, the scholarship he eventually received helped his college-educated parents finance his education, but football always came second to school—despite the fact that it was far more time-consuming. This message, he shared, was instilled at home and never escaped him.

The majority of his teammates, on the other hand, were not as fortunate. For the most part, they arrived less prepared, less financially stable, and more dependent on the flawed notion that fully investing in sports was their best chance to help themselves, and by extension, their families. Almost all the guys on the team, including John, believed they had a chance to play professionally; however, when John fell down the depth chart as a sophomore, he shifted gears to focus on improving his grades and finding internships to prepare for the real world. In his estimation, this reprioritizing was the most important decision he could have made. The rest of the guys, by contrast, came in with an "NFL-or-bust" mentality and sacrificed everything to make those dreams come true. What John found most disheartening was that his teammates did not have anyone to help them understand when it was time to reprioritize. By the time they realized it, it was too late.

At present, college sports lack equity. As in so many sectors of life, we are trapped in a survival-of-the-fittest mindset regarding who can achieve the most within the dual and dueling school and sport dichotomy. Though all student-athletes do not have the same capacity to achieve academic success while pursuing athletic excellence, most do have the capacity for high achievement in both if provided a more equitable framework. This framework may differ considerably from the systems that exist today, but a variety of paths are necessary to provide all student-athletes with a fair chance to earn a meaningful degree and secure employment after college. That variety is what educators, policymakers, and sports insiders need to pursue. In this book, we offer you our thinking on those paths to success.

Equity recognizes that student-athletes have varying capabilities and desires regarding athletic and academic success as they enter college and throughout their journey. One size, in terms of reforms, will not fit all. The system of college sports must take these students as they are. And in many cases, they currently are. What's missing, though, is the next step: providing a set of nontraditional paths to meaningful degree completion. Recognizing diversity of backgrounds and interests, this book focuses on aiding the largest number of student-athletes to achieve academic success.

Today, as the revenues generated by big-time college sports continue to skyrocket, the dominant discourse surrounds whether student-athletes should be paid for play. These conversations begin at the highest level, Division I, where student-athletes garner massive publicity, foster school pride, provide entertainment, and generate billions of dollars from ticket sales, merchandise, and television rights contracts. Nevertheless, the NCAA's long judicially upheld amateurism principle prevents student-athletes from receiving any compensation beyond scholarships equal to room, board, tuition, educational fees, and the cost of attendance. These rules have recently been relaxed in the expansion of the cost of attendance category, but the fact remains that many of the student-athletes competing for some of the richest athletics departments in the country are struggling to get by.

Meanwhile, coaches, athletic directors, conference officials, and other NCAA stakeholders are making incredibly lucrative salaries. In 39 of 50 states, the highest-paid public employee is either a football coach or a men's basketball coach.[4] Ironically, the contracts for coaches and other administrators are no longer filled with bonuses only for wins on the field, but now include bonuses for the academic success of their respective athletes. While coaches and athletic directors may be compensated for their players' hard work, the players themselves don't have the same right. Additionally, while the incentive to encourage the academic success of students is a good thing, an inherent problem is the sometimes opportunistic and inappropriate behavior that may be encouraged by these adults supervising young student-athletes, ranging from choosing less rigorous majors to taking sham courses.[5] These nuanced incentives ought to be explored in greater detail. The focus remains, perhaps understandably so, on compensation for athletes. This approach, of course, is a flawed one. Not all student-athletes need the money, but all can benefit from an education that leads to a meaningful degree and employment.

This is not to say that academics has not been a part of the conversation; to varying degrees, it has been. However, the pay-for-play debates have long eclipsed academic efforts focused on raising graduation rates. For example, the most widely cited works critiquing college sports, from Taylor Branch's 2011 *Atlantic* article "The Shame of College Sports" to Joe Nocera's 2016 book *Indentured: The Inside Story of the Rebellion against the NCAA*, pay little attention to college completion. Even less attention is given to the quality of education and the value of the degrees these athletes receive. While we have no problem with greater compensation, we maintain the worthier goal is prioritizing *meaningful* education. Greater compensation begins in the classroom.

This book strives to provoke a paradigm shift in both what we discuss about college sports and how the existing system should be reformed to better serve student-athletes and society—to take these young people as they are and systematically provide the framework to make them academically stronger. Paying them is not the magic bullet. Even while we acknowledge the exceptional amount of time and commitment college athletes must commit to be successful in their respective sports, we contend that all who touch college sport—including the athletes themselves—should elevate the granting of degrees to *at least* equal status with institutional, financial, and athletic success. It is important to be clear that, as much attention will be cast in its direction in this book, this is not an issue for the NCAA to tackle alone. Using that entity as a punching bag is a dated approach to this problem. The reality is that, although it is often on the wrong end of many lawsuits and complaints, the NCAA as an organization is searching for the right path to reform as well. Redirecting that enterprise is, in fact, like redirecting the *Enterprise*.

As we assert that the reform agenda should be more concerned with academic goals than economic goals, we also place strategic focus on improving the quality of education, not just the rates at which student-athletes graduate. As Jesse Washington explained in his 2017 article "Big-Time College Athletes Should Be Paid with Big-Time Educations,"[6] we should be making sure college athletes are getting real educations before we discuss paying them.

We recognize that nothing is universal, and even today, the degree is not the best answer for all. Yes, life can be fine, even exceptional, without a college degree. The list of notable tech dropouts, musicians, and one-and-done professional athletes is legion. Key here, however, is that the group of individuals we are focused on are in college—even if only for a one-and-done year—and have the opportunity to accomplish something meaningful, even if via a non-traditional manner. Further, the data shows those who hold college degrees are more likely to be successful and to positively impact society.[7] We cautiously note the exceptions. As Woodson wrote in *The Mis-education of the Negro* back in 1933:

> In the schools of business administration, Negroes are trained exclusively in the psychology and economics of Wall Street and are, therefore, made to despise the opportunities to run ice wagons, push banana carts, and sell peanuts among their own people. Foreigners who have not studied economics but have studied Negroes, take up this business and grow rich.[8]

Here, Woodson pushes back against convention and monolithic thinking, conveying the message that a degree alone may not be the answer for a given individual or situation. In essence, one can be *mis-educated* even with a degree. This is why counseling, a key component of our model, plays such an important role in the reform agenda.

We are also flexible as to what constitutes what we refer to throughout as a *meaningful* degree. This is not the venue where the merits of a tech versus business versus liberal arts or any other degree are being undertaken. In fact, what constitutes "meaningful" varies for student-athletes as individuals in the same manner that it varies for any other students. In that sense, we do not give the epigraph to this chapter a full-throated endorsement in its literal sense, but we certainly do in terms of its message. If the investment in time is made to earn a degree, it should be a degree that delivers value to the individual, not to the school, the NCAA, or federal government graduation rate statistics. We simply add the modifier so that no one mistakes that we would be supportive of the granting of sham or other nonimpactful, useless degrees.

For reform to happen, as we later detail, college sport needs a *constructive disrupter* or *disrupters* with a destination and goal. With the goal of improving the quality and quantity of student-athletes' degrees, we present a manifesto.

The Student-Athlete Manifesto

Parsing out reforms into three sections (actions, facilitators, and administration), the Student-Athlete Manifesto seeks the following:

Actions

1) Make obtaining a *meaningful* degree the priority—*not* football, basketball, or any sport.
2) Broaden the pathway to meaningful degree completion by granting athletes the right to return to complete the degree, including one-and-done athletes.

Facilitators

3) Mandate academic boot camps for entering student-athletes and professional boot camps for exiting student-athletes.
4) Make maximum use of summers for educational and professional development.

5) Expand the opportunity to get credits from institutions offering online opportunities.
6) Provide personalized counseling on the best paths among academic and career options.

Administration

7) Review and enforce existing limits on hours of sports participation.
8) Enhance, but more closely monitor, tutoring support.
9) Make sure athletes are the ones actually doing the academic work.
10) More stringently prohibit athlete-only or athlete-dominant courses.
11) Standardize a way to more accurately track all graduation rates.
12) Establish independently administered pre- and posttests to truly measure learning.
13) Increase accountability by requiring the NCAA to routinely report this data disaggregated by race, sex, sport, division, and particular subsets of institutions within a division (i.e., the Power 5 conferences).

The Book's Roadmap

The goal of our book is to guide the reader through our manifesto and contemplate the disruptive forces that can bring about change in college sports. Chapter 1, "Money and College Sports," outlines the relevant elements of the amateurism journey and the increased infusion of cash via media rights deals that have changed the college sports landscape and created immense tension between athletic and academic priorities. We want the reader to be clear on the changing economics that have set the stage for the massive change that is under way. Chapter 2, "The Miseducation of the Student-Athlete," compares the hopeful NCAA graduation data against the troubling academic and employment outcomes reported by independent researchers. Firsthand accounts, like the quote at the beginning of our introduction, are peppered throughout the manuscript, painting a unique picture of how revenue-athletes—most often football, men's basketball, and sometimes women's basketball players—experience college differently than their peers. Chapter 3, "Time for Change?," looks at the previous attempts at student-athlete compensation reform, including the one-sided Ivy and professional models, and explains why they haven't gained much traction. It concludes by proposing that, rather than severing athletics and academics, we reframe the compensation discourse around the idea of ensuring that all student-athletes reap more of college's benefits. Chapter 4, "The Solution: Constructive, Disruptive Systemic Change," explains how to best use increased revenues to benefit student-athletes. It lays out impactful programs for athletes prior to their arrival on campus, during their time there, and after they leave their respective institutions. This will range from preparatory and tutorial programs to funds for the return to college following their attempts at professional careers. Chapter 5, "Moving toward Change and Implementing Solutions," looks at the mechanics of how these changes might be made. It then explores what it would take to actually implement the recommended changes and who would have to make them. At the end, we leave you to contemplate our Student-Athlete Manifesto and Meaningful Degree Model and the broader societal impact if the status quo continues.

Chapter 1

Money and College Sports

People are playing for jobs and bonuses. I think it's a part of the
story, and we try to act like it's not. It should be educationally
driven. I 100% agree with that. It should be, but it's not. Guess
what? I can recite a million lines of Shakespeare, and that's not
going to make the school multiple billions of dollars. But if I can
get ten sacks in a season, put a jersey number in the bookstore,
and create more exposure and money . . . It trickles down. It's all
about money. That's why it's not an amateur sport.[9]

T wo great college sports powers prepare to do battle. Ever-loyal
fans are bombarded by messages from sponsors on their way
into and during the event. They tolerate the abundant messaging
knowing the competition is going to be entertaining and advertising
is simply a part of the price, in addition to admission, they pay to
enjoy the festivities. In fact, the alums know those advertising dollars will ultimately benefit their alma mater. On this particular game
day, there is a hint of scandal, as there are murmurs and rumblings
about the eligibility of one of the players on the field. Nonetheless,
the fans want to see him compete. He is a great athlete, after all. More
on this familiar scene in a moment.

Due to the recent onslaught of lawsuits involving the NCAA and
amateurism, some of the stories around the roots of ethics in college
sport are not new. By now most who follow sport know that the past

common conceptions of amateurism are false. In both *O'Bannon v. NCAA*, which focused on athlete likeness and image rights, and *Jenkins v. NCAA*, which decided whether the fixed compensation NCAA athletes receive violates antitrust laws, amateurism and money were the driving issues. The dispute about amateurism in NCAA sport is now such a part of popular culture that even casual observers have opinions.

But the problems inherent in college sport that go beyond amateurism and money are not new either. The scenario described in the opening paragraphs of this chapter is not a big-time modern-day football rivalry or bowl game, but rather a sporting battle from nearly two centuries ago. In 1852, a savvy businessman named James Elkins paid two schools—Harvard and Yale—to compete in a boat race as a means of promoting the hotel he built along his famous Boston, Concord, and Montreal railroad line. Desperate to beat their rivals from New Haven in this fancy eight-day boat race, Harvard hired a professional boatman and disguised him as a student. All the while, the wealthy attendees drank and gambled on the outcome.[10]

From the very start, companies have used college sports to advertise their services, just as teams have bent the rules on academically eligible athletes.[11] And of course, from the beginning, scandals surrounding the money involved in intercollegiate athletics have distracted us from focusing on whether student-athletes graduate and whether the degrees they earn are of any use. Simply, cheating, sponsorship, and academic fraud have plagued college sports from the outset.

Why hasn't the popular discourse been more focused on this student achievement issue? In this chapter, we address the contradictions at the core of college sports, detailing the myth of amateurism, the origin of the term "student-athlete," and the NCAA-supported transitions to professionalism and commercialism. At the core, we ask, With the infusion of cash, shouldn't we step back and reprioritize college sport spending for the greater good? Specifically, the greater good being college degrees that provide the springboard for a life beyond sport.

The Myth of Amateurism

Broadly speaking, we are in our current state because college sport did not grow out of the typical American capitalist model. Indeed, in a sense, college sport has been a uniquely regulated sector of our society. Despite being shrouded in mythology, the amateur ideal has always been about money, so in that sense capitalism is omnipresent.

During the Middle Ages, the emergence of residential colleges increased the amount of free time European students had, and that time was eventually filled with games. As British campuses were reserved for the elite, so too were the competitive sports played on them. Wealthy and unconcerned with profit, the gentleman-aristocrat of those times participated in sports merely for "the love of the game." By contrast, because the working class might use sports for personal gain and may have had an advantage because their vocation involved physical labor, the elite used the guise of amateurism to keep them out. The rich avoided investing too much time, effort, or energy into a single activity. For them, sport was a hobby, and by no means was it to be considered a central focus.[12]

Though few were aristocrats in England, American colonists adopted many of their customs. By the Revolutionary War in 1776, over two dozen British sports were embedded in the budding American culture. Organized by students, campus athletics, which took root in the middle of the 19th century, continued in the amateur spirit. It is commonly noted that the first "official" game of college football took place between Rutgers and Princeton in 1868, but games similar to American football had been played on college campuses for years before that. These collegiate sports were instantly popular, and over time, most northeastern schools recognized their importance in the campus experience and created departments dedicated entirely to physical activity. Supported by colleges, competitive sports grew into an obsession.[13]

By the turn of the century, college football was too popular, corrupt, and dangerous to ignore. After 21 deaths and 200 injuries in the

1904 season alone, university presidents and faculty were not just looking to reform college football, but calling for its outright termination. In order to restore, or some would argue instill, positive conduct, president Theodore Roosevelt invited select leaders in the game to a White House conference in 1905. A football admirer and strong believer in amateurism, Roosevelt believed that no student who had ever been compensated for his athletic ability should be allowed to participate in college sport.[14] As player deaths and corruption continued, New York University (NYU) chancellor Henry MacCracken convened a national conference to decide whether football could be reformed or should be eliminated altogether.[15]

This larger meeting resulted in the creation of a Rules Committee. Later that year, representatives from both the White House and NYU conferences met to formally establish a set of firm college football rules. The Intercollegiate Athletic Association, renamed the National Collegiate Athletic Association (NCAA) in 1910, was formed as a regulatory body to ensure both fairness and safety. The amateur ideal adopted from the British aristocracy was among its founding principles.[16]

Notably, the primary language then, as it is now, was not about academics. Little in the rules implemented at the time had anything to do with student-athletes earning degrees; rather, the focus was on safety and amateurism. In retrospect, then, at its very formation, we can make the case that collegiate football, and by extension collegiate sports, had no real plan to assist the key participants in accomplishing what now has proved to be one of the most difficult tasks in the academy: to play sport at the highest level and also earn a meaningful degree.

From Amateurs to Professionals, 1910–1984

The next 70 years saw the powers that be in college sport embrace, albeit reluctantly, the unique form of "amateur" sport we see today. This was also the era when the greatest struggle to understand the role of academics in this enterprise was, without positive outcome, contemplated.

In the beginning, the NCAA actually played a minor role in the governing of college sports. For the first 20 years, students remained in control, as they had been from the earliest days of college sport and were rarely, if ever, monitored by faculty. In the 1920s, the arrival of radio broadcasts of games, the building of stadiums, and the spreading of college football to the south and west allowed for greater fan interest. The game became a nationwide sensation. The 1927 Rose Bowl, which pitted Stanford against Alabama, was the first-ever coast-to-coast US radio broadcast, turning college athletes into local, regional, and national heroes.[17]

College sport's rapid growth also opened it up to more criticism. A national debate over whether college athletes should be paid was launched in 1929 when a Carnegie Foundation report revealed that out of 112 schools surveyed, 81 of them had recruited athletes and paid them in a variety of prohibited ways, from disguised booster funds and illegal athletic scholarships called "subsidies" to no-show jobs.[18] The discussion would return to the forefront in 1939, when first-year athletes at the University of Pittsburgh actually went on strike because their upperclassmen teammates were getting paid more than them. That report raised, without resolution, the question of why college sport existed as this unique extension of the American collegiate system. Many, for the first time, came to realize that the phenomena of sport associated with college campuses was uniquely American. Few, however, fully grasped that there were no rules or precedents as to what an enterprise like this should look like, or what it should prioritize. It was, especially then, a shrouded mush of capitalism, amateurism, and somewhere in there, education. With no precedent to follow, it is easy to look back and understand why so many mistakes were made.

By 1946, the NCAA had grown so embarrassed by its inability to handle bribery, rampant gambling, and recruitment scandals that it again assembled conference officials to develop a code of ethics. Note that although the education of athletes was a matter of concern, the focus of reform was on minimizing scandal. Seeking to reach a compromise between the southern schools in favor of full athletic scholarships and the Ivy League schools that called for all students to be treated the same, the Sanity Code prohibited schools from compensating athletes beyond free tuition and meals. This 1948 legislation marked the first official step toward professionalism.[19] The amateur ideal, as it existed among the British aristocracy, had been lost. The last vestige of a sporting model was dispensed and the formal creation of today's priorities was under way. The concept of moving from the British aristocratic model was not the problem; rather, it was the lack of framing of the transition to be in the best interest of those participants who would come to be known as student-athletes.

During the 1950s, the NCAA began to flex its muscle, replacing the Sanity Code with the Committee on Infractions and appointing Walter Byers as its first executive director. Byers and the Committee on Infractions were tested almost immediately, as two major scandals—one involving grade counterfeiting in football and another involving point shaving and gambling in basketball—rocked college sports in 1951.[20] Their responses set major precedents. The committee handed the University of Kentucky and iconic head basketball coach Adolph Rupp the first-ever "death penalty," barring the Wildcats from competition for the entire 1952 season.[21] This moment displayed the power the NCAA possessed, and for the first time was beginning to wield. The NCAA as boogeyman was born. In some sense, this was when public criticism shifted too much to this entity rather than to the existing and growing problems within the endeavor.

The Birth of the Term "Student-Athlete"

Perhaps Byers' most salient win was the legal battle leading to the creation of the term "student-athlete." When Ray Dennison, a Fort Lewis A&M Aggies football player, died of a head injury, his wife tried to sue the NCAA for the workmen's compensation death benefit.

In a quick but calculated response, the NCAA placed the word "student" in front of "athlete" to (1) emphasize players' status as students, (2) prevent them from being identified as employees, and (3) promote the amateur ideal of academics over athletics.[22] By preserving the image of college athletes as students first, athletes second, and employees never, the phrase has been an extremely effective defense in court. By defining students who participate in sports in college as different from others in the student body, the term further distracts from the focus on degree completion. It is important to be clear that the creation of the student-athlete terminology was not a refocusing of the college sports enterprise but a shielding of its operations from lawsuits.

The NCAA quickly transformed into a self-sustaining bureaucracy under Byers. The revenue generated by televising college football's "Game of the Week" ballooned after the NCAA forced football powerhouses the University of Pennsylvania and the University of Notre Dame out of their independent television deals. In 1952, Byers' maneuvering resulted in NBC paying the NCAA $1.14 million for a restricted football package, enough to move the expanding organization from a shared space with the Big Ten conference in Chicago to its own new headquarters in Kansas City, Missouri.[23] By the mid-1950s, the NCAA's men's basketball tournament had become the sport's premier invitational tournament, overcoming competition from the rival National Invitation Tournament.[24] It became increasingly profitable with the expansion to 48 teams in 1975, and in 1979, the storied rivalry between Indiana State's Larry Bird and Michigan State's Magic Johnson turned the tournament into a national phenomenon. The $100,000 the NCAA made in basketball revenue in 1947 reached $500,000 in 1967, $1 million in 1972, and $22 million in 1981.[25] Throughout the 1970s, the growing interest in and profitability of college sports increased the NCAA's enforcement capacity so much that it was accused of unfairly exercising its power. To address these concerns, the NCAA added checks and balances, separating its member institutions into three competitively similar groups called divisions.

The Commercial Enterprise of Big-Time College Sports (1984 to the present)

Television watching as a national pastime, the value of broadcasting deals, and the popularity of college basketball increased significantly throughout the 1980s and 1990s. As gambling and the introduction of the point spread made basketball even more popular, NCAA officials quickly realized it was cheaper and easier to broadcast than football—and looked to maximize their profits. In 1984, CBS paid a staggering $1 billion for exclusive broadcasting rights for the sport.[26] Commercialism had officially become one of the NCAA's primary goals; simultaneously, those soaring profits served as an indicator of the entity's "success."

Commercialism reached new heights as cable television, major athletic conferences, and ESPN attempted to satisfy the limitless appetites of sports fans, scheduling day and night games throughout the week and on weekends. In 1999, CBS renegotiated broadcasting rights for the tournament, paying the NCAA $6 billion over 11 years, or approximately $550 million annually.[27] By drastically increasing the value of college sports, basketball swiftly went from a minor to a major consideration. What academics had feared all along was confirmed: Whoever makes the money makes the rules.

The soaring costs of coaching salaries, athletic department spending, and television rights packages evidence how commercial big-time college sport has become. More telling than the $5 million, $7 million, and $10 million (yes, $10 million) salaries that Michigan, Alabama, and Duke pay head coaches Jim Harbaugh, Nick Saban, and Mike Krzyzewski, respectively, is the $772 million that 48 universities in the Power 5 conferences spent on athletic facilities alone in 2014.[28] Further, in 2016, just six years after entering into a 14-year, $10.8 billion agreement to broadcast the Division I Men's Basketball Championship, the NCAA and Turner/CBS sports signed an eight-year $8.8 billion extension.[29]

Recent years have also seen the value of media-rights deals to individual conferences skyrocket as well. This has come about not just because of the payout each receives as part of the March Madness revenue, but also because of the massive influx of money earned from television rights for conference games and each league's share of the College Football Playoff deal.

The "Sanity Code" moment of this era of soaring revenues was a report issued by the Knight Commission in 1991. Headed by the former presidents of the University of Notre Dame and the University of North Carolina system, the commission took a rare, broad-based view of the college athletics enterprise—and concluded, rather harshly, that the situation was out of control. In an expression of despair, if not outright desperation, the commission noted that nothing had changed since the Carnegie report issued six decades earlier, and called for university presidents—not athletic directors, boosters, or the NCAA—to finally take control of college athletics.

It would hardly have been outrageous for anyone to think at the time, Well, who has been in charge all along?

Conclusion

Though the student-athlete and amateur ideals claim to prioritize academic success over athletic achievement, college sport has evolved into a mainstream entertainment business where universities compete for money and exposure as much as they do for victories. Division I men's basketball and football have become highly commercial—certainly run as ruthlessly as any other multibillion-dollar business enterprise—and as a result have facilitated the professionalization of college athletic conferences. The Big Ten, for example, provides more sport content for television than many popular professional leagues.

The sports media, especially the television media, have increased the demand for big-time college sports, which ultimately pushed the NCAA to lengthen the football season and create the College Football Playoff in order to maximize profits. Growing financial pressures have contributed to a win-at-all-costs mentality, leading to negative perceptions of some athletics programs. In the past decade, more than half the institutions playing at the most competitive level were sanctioned for violating NCAA regulations.[30]

Rather than achieving systematic reform, the NCAA has developed a complex code of conduct that focuses primarily on the athlete's ability (or lack thereof) to profit from her on-the-field success; the focus, as always, is on maintaining the NCAA-defined vision of amateurism. Almost always lost in those rules is the idea of helping athletes earn a meaningful degree. An underlying assumption is that cheating by parties in the enterprise is likely to occur unless the principle of amateurism is adhered to.

As the maze of regulations misses meaningful degree goals, the reform agenda has failed to ease the commercial pressures creating tension between athletics and academics. Thus, amateurism not only exploits athletes financially but also undermines educational integrity. While many continue to debate whether student-athletes should be compensated, we hope to shift the discussion to how well they are being educated. In the next chapter, we discuss the academic and employment outcomes for student-athletes.

Chapter 2

The Miseducation of the Student-Athlete

I went to a very good institution in terms of academics. Up until this quarter, the second half of my senior year, I never had a close relationship with any of my professors, never really went to office hours, and my grades suffered immensely. It's not because I was slacking. My GPA isn't terrible, it's just not what it could be. I did what I had to do to get the grades to be able to play. The grades, relationships with professors, job opportunities . . . you just can't make the most of them like normal students can. If you're playing DI [Division I] football, you're just not going to get the same academically. I definitely didn't get out of [the university] what most people do.[31]

While the account above is on one end of the miseducation spectrum, the story that follows is on the other. After four years of playing basketball for Creighton, a Jesuit school in Omaha, Nebraska, Kevin Ross was functionally illiterate. As an athlete, he floated through the Kansas school system, eventually accepting an athletic scholarship offer in 1978. In 1982, having never been held academically accountable, the 23-year-old left the university reading at a second-grade level. Kevin would have to return to elementary school to learn what he didn't the first time around. At six foot, nine inches, he sat in the eighth-grade classroom of Westside Preparatory School's legendary educator, Marva Collins, struggling to write a check and read a menu. In 1989, Ross sued Creighton, alleging that he fulfilled his contracts in playing basketball for the school, while the school failed to fulfill its promise of educating him. Though myriad reforms have taken place since, the Kevin Ross story remains a cautionary tale in the miseducation hall of shame. Avoiding outcomes like this is what college sport leadership must do.

Under the NCAA's governance, more than 1,120 schools, 19,500 teams, and 460,000 student-athletes[32] compete across 24 sports in three like-minded divisions (Divisions I, II, and III).[33] The association notes that college sports engage students, improve academic performance, help develop transferable skills, foster physical fitness, provide opportunities to display their diverse skills, and prepare them for life.[34] Simultaneously, and in direct contrast to those positives, decades of research assert that college sports distract students from educationally purposeful activities, distort academic values, perpetuate dependence and conformity, pacify spectators, deprive educational programs of resources, and subject athletes to injury and isolation in culturally hostile campus climates.[35] On *second* blush those two determinations are not as contradictory as they might seem. Many students are successful. Degree completion occurs more often than not. Many of life's great lessons are learned. But at the same time, some student-athletes are not successful, are not focused, could use more time, miss out on much of student life, and certainly more often than not, do not have the professional athletic career they expected would be there once their college career was over.

Chapter 2 takes a closer look at the inconsistencies between NCAA data and independent research with the goal of identifying the areas of college sports most in need of reform. Ultimately, this chapter highlights the differing academic and professional outcomes that lead to our focus on meaningful degree attainment. It also concludes that, in a sense, both schools of thought noted at the beginning of the chapter are correct, but regardless, the pathways to provide success to greater numbers must be expanded.

Research on the campus experiences of student-athletes remained scarce until 1990, when concerns about their learning and personal development, particularly those playing Division I football and men's basketball, caused the NCAA and the federal government to require colleges and universities to report all student graduation rates. As the ultimate goal of attending college is to get a degree, graduation rates would ideally provide a 1:1 comparison of success for athletes and nonathletes and measure the impact of participation in college sport. There is a simple baseline question that many would think has an easy answer: Does participation in sport harm or help academic performance? More specifically, do sports negatively impact the receipt of meaningful degrees? For several reasons, even the basic measurement between the student-athlete and the non-student-athlete is not as straightforward as one would desire. Here's why.

First, when the initial global measurements were undertaken, the student-athlete graduation rates were separated by race, gender, and sport, but not by division. This shortcoming allowed claims such as "student-athlete graduation rates consistently surpass those of their student-body counterparts,"[36] because data in the aggregate hides the underperformance of the athletes at the most lucrative and competitive level, Division I. That statement is certainly factually accurate, but it's also deeply misleading.

Second, the federal graduation rate fails to account for student-athletes who transfer into an institution after their first year and counts students who transfer out as dropouts, regardless of whether they complete their degrees elsewhere.[37] Accordingly, the NCAA created its own measures in 2002—the graduation success rate (GSR) for Division I and the academic success rate (ASR) for Division II and Division III. The federal graduation rate is believed to *underestimate* graduation numbers, while the GSR and the ASR are critiqued for *overestimating* them. With no GSR or ASR for the general student body, there exists no data with which we can directly compare the graduation rates of student-athletes and their nonsport peers.

Finally, data reported by the NCAA, if reviewed in a vacuum, is often inconsistent with decades of published research. Though graduation rates are getting better, the frequency of academic scandals[38] in the past decade alone suggests that a clear understanding of the academic benefits of participating in college sports remains a mystery. Scandals such as the one still being investigated at the University of North Carolina cast serious doubt on the actual levels of success. How many of the degrees being granted are tainted? What else is going on that statistics alone do not uncover?

NCAA Data

Graduation rates are used, broadly speaking, to assess whether athletic programs are upholding the school's academic ideals. Since the NCAA began tracking them in 1983, the graduation rates of student-athletes have steadily increased. For 25 years, student-athletes across all three divisions have been outperforming their nonathlete peers in the classroom and more frequently completing their degree.[39] Figure 1 highlights the rise in graduation rates between 2002 and 2016.

Beyond graduation rate data, the NCAA has produced a number of reports addressing a variety of issues in college sport. Part of the "Behind the Blue Disk" series, *Student-Athlete Benefits* is a one-page document, issued in 2013, that summarizes the immediate and lifelong benefits of participating in intercollegiate athletics.[40] The report contends that student-athletes are afforded additional pathways to a college education through athletic scholarships; receive academic support and tutoring services; have access to elite training opportunities, a healthy diet, and $70 million in emergency resources through the NCAA's Student Assistance Fund; are provided medical insurance through their schools; gain exposure and have new experiences as they travel for competition; and are prepared for life after college having learned transferable skills such as time management, leadership, and teamwork.[41]

Conducted in 2006, 2010, and again in 2015, *GOALS (Growth, Opportunities, Aspirations and Learning of Students in College)* is a study of the experiences and well-being of current student-athletes designed to provide data to NCAA committees, policymakers, and member institutions. The range of issues examined include athletic,

Figure 1: Graduation Rates on the Rise

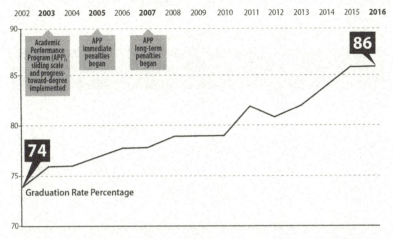

Source: NCAA, "Graduation Rates," 2017, http://www.ncaa.org/about/resources/research/graduation-rates

academic, and social experiences, as well as recruitment, time commitments, on-campus support, finances, and health and well-being.
Again, the academic findings set forth are overwhelmingly optimistic. More than three-quarters of current student-athletes report
that their overall academic experience has been positive. As seen in
Table 1, the majority report feeling positive about their ability to keep
up with their classes while in-season (~60% in Division I, 65% in
Division II, 70% in Division III). Additionally, more than two-thirds
report that they have developed at least one close personal relationship with faculty, and more than 80% say they believe their coach
cares whether they graduate.[42]

Most recently, the NCAA commissioned Gallup to conduct a
study on life after college to assess the long-term effects of participating in intercollegiate athletics. *Understanding Life Outcomes of
Former NCAA Student-Athletes* compares five areas of well-being for
former student-athletes and their nonsport peers: purpose, social,
community, physical, and financial. Student-athletes who completed

Table 1: Student-Athlete Opportunities

How do you feel about your ability to keep up with your classes in-season?

(% responding Positive or Very Positive)

Baseball	Men's Basketball	Football FBS	FCS*	Men's Other	Women's Basketball	Women's Other
Division I						
56%	62%	60%	55%	60%	56%	61%
Division II						
63%	58%	63%		67%	62%	63%
Division III						
64%	74%	68%		71%	67%	74%

* Football Bowl Subdivision (FBS) and Football Championship Subdivision (FCS)

Source: NCAA, "Growth, Opportunities, Aspirations and Learning of Students in College (GOALS) Study," 2015, http://www.ncaa.org/about/resources/research/ncaa-goals-study

their bachelor's degree between 1970 and 2014 are more likely than non-student-athletes to like and be motivated by their jobs, have loving and supportive relationships, enjoy and feel safe engaging with the community they live in, and be in good physical health.[43] They are also just as likely to be as financially secure as their non-student-athlete peers; 82% of them are employed at their desired level.

Former student-athletes in this study also reported not having missed out on key college experiences, despite the immense time commitment college sports require. Finally, they reported having a professor who cared about them as a person, actively engaging in their campus communities during college, and participating in clubs and organizations as well as fraternities and sororities at higher rates than their non-student-athlete counterparts.[44] The vast majority of NCAA data paints a positive picture of college sports' impact on academics and life outcomes by focusing on the overall successes; however, disaggregated data tells a different story.

Disaggregating the Data

Amid steadily rising overall graduation rates, the prevalence of academic scandals has caused independent researchers to question the extent to which Division I student-athletes are actually benefitting from participation in college sports relative to their nonsport, Division 2, and Division 3 peers. From lower admission standards to grade inflation and so-called paper classes, the historic and contemporary ethical compromises made to field winning teams at the most competitive levels have been consistently reported over the years.[45] Hence, the calls for transparency have resulted in data disaggregated by sport, race, gender, and division, revealing what many have suspected: long-standing and pervasive inequities, especially in revenue-generating programs.[46] For example, the NCAA's claim that "student-athlete graduation rates consistently surpass those of their student-body counterparts"[47] does not hold true in Division I men's basketball and Football Bowl Subdivision (FBS) football. The proper perspective on this data is that for the vast majority of student-athletes, there is a higher level of academic success than for those students who are not athletes. The more intense and elite the athletic activity—as is frankly logical—the more difficult it is to be successful in a traditional academic program.

This is an important qualifier, of course, as one contemplates the data. It can be argued that the individuals most likely to make the largest academic sacrifices for athletic success are those who believe they may play professionally. The more elite the opportunity, the more one must, in a sense, be positioned for athletic failure if playing professionally is a goal. Subsequently, providing a path that allows athletes to shift their focus to academics after exhausting their athletic opportunities may be a necessary solution.

When the data is separated, accountability is achievable and key areas of improvement are more easily identifiable. Consider the aforementioned GOALS study. As seen in Table 2, while over a third of student-athletes said that athletic participation prevented them from taking desired classes, the numbers are even higher in Division I,

Table 2: Student-Athlete Majors

Has athletics participation prevented you from majoring in what you really want?

	Baseball	Men's Basketball	Football FBS	FCS	Men's Other	Women's Basketball	Women's Other
Division I							
Yes, but I do not have regrets	24%	22%	25%	21%	18%	25%	21%
Yes, and I have regrets about my major choice	8%	7%	11%	7%	5%	7%	4%
Division II							
Yes, but I do not have regrets	17%	20%	14%		11%	20%	13%
Yes, and I have regrets about my major choice	4%	6%	4%		2%	4%	3%
Division III							
Yes, but I do not have regrets	8%	9%	9%		6%	9%	7%
Yes, and I have regrets about my major choice	1%	2%	2%		1%	1%	1%

Up 5% or more from 2010

Source: NCAA, "Growth, Opportunities, Aspirations and Learning of Students in College (GOALS) Study," 2015, http://www.ncaa.org/about/resources/research/ncaa-goals-study

where student-athletes more frequently indicated sports prevented them from enrolling in their desired *major*. Interestingly, most of the participants who changed courses and majors report not regretting their choices. This makes sense, however, as current students have yet to see the long-term impact of these changes. It remains to be seen how they will feel a decade or two later. Chief among our proposed reforms is student-athletes' ability to pursue their desired degrees. And if not their "dream" degree—many students change and evolve for various reasons once they begin to move forward in their studies—then at the very least a meaningful degree, not one that was selected for them simply so that she or he could remain eligible.

Other activities that are central to the college experience are also often out of reach for high-level student-athletes. For instance, while 10% of Division I athletes will have the opportunity to study abroad, 33% of them report wanting to participate but being unable to because of their athletic commitments. Additionally, while most student-athletes aspire to intern, only one-third of Division I baseball, basketball, and football players are able to because of the demands of high-level sport.[48]

Of course, participation in any sport brings with it a certain level of commitment. The question to ask is whether there are methods to provide the athlete with more time to make the most of both their athletic and academic careers. One path is to be intentional about extending the length of athletic scholarships. We find it critically important that student-athletes, after their eligibility has expired, be granted additional years for study and career preparation, whether on campus, online, or some combination of both. Decades of research documenting the problematic outcomes for elite student-athletes concur: The absence of these developmental experiences renders a degree less valuable.

The Revenue-Athlete Experience

The literature on Division I student-athletes routinely argues that the problematic academic, psychosocial, and career development outcomes they experience are a function of the institutions' inability to engage them in meaningful extracurricular activities beyond sports.[49]

Time Management

Revenue-athletes are student-athletes who participate in sports that generate revenue, namely, men's basketball and football. They represent a unique subset of the college population for whom success requires putting in hard work, showing dedication, and performing in the classroom as well as on the field or court. Beyond balancing the academic and social demands that their nonathlete peers do, they must also manage a bevy of exhaustive athletic demands, including traveling, practicing, and competing.[50] When their sports are in season, for example, student-athletes typically far exceed the maximum limit of 20 hours per week on sport-related activities, miss several classes, and endure bodily injury and fatigue.[51] Even keeping track of the complex set of rules and requirements the NCAA and athletic conferences mandate for intercollegiate athletic eligibility can be time-consuming and arduous. In a 2006 national study on their perceptions of their college experience, the majority of participants expressed the desire to spend more time on academics and pursue more professional and educational opportunities, such as internships and research with faculty. However, 80% of the respondents cited the demands of their sport as the main reason they were unable to pursue those other interests. Fittingly, 62% of student-athletes reported participation in intercollegiate athletics contributed to them viewing themselves more as athletes than as students.[52]

Complex Roles and Identities

Among revenue-athletes' greatest challenges is balancing competing social, academic, and athletic roles.[53] At the NCAA's most competitive, lucrative, and popular level, Division I athletes receive elevated levels of social reinforcement for their athletic identities and disproportionately less for any others. Because these athletes are glorified by society for their athletic prowess, their concept of self is heavily influenced by the daily face-to-face campus interactions in which they are expected to live up to this media-created celebrity persona.[54] Naturally, they begin to privilege their athletic roles and responsibilities above their roles as students, as team practices, conditioning, games, and travel engulf their time and ultimately their identities. As they primarily live, eat, socialize, and take classes with teammates and other athletes, student-athletes are afforded limited opportunities to engage with nonathlete peers. Resultantly, they become entrenched in a separate subculture that discourages expending effort in academic activities, distracts them from studying, and compels them to disassociate with other students who could provide greater academic role modeling.[55] Sometimes the overwhelmingly demanding athletic role, the prioritization of athletics over academics, the resulting academic frustrations, and the lack of positive reinforcement causes players to reduce their academic identity or drop it entirely. In some cases, the premature commitment of revenue-athletes to their sporting identity eliminates any opportunity for them to meaningfully explore others, such as career exploration, talent development, or joining social clubs or interest groups.[56] Essentially, the very nature of their athletic commitment vastly undermines their ability to fully integrate into the larger campus community and be academically successful. This primary hurdle must be overcome for any real change in academic outcomes to occur.

The "Dumb Jock" Stereotype

Revenue-athletes must also contend with the preconceived notions regarding their academic capabilities. At colleges and universities with high-profile sports programs, student-athletes are also often subject to the pervasive "dumb jock" stereotype. Cast in that role and assumed to be incapable of performing well in the classroom, they are stigmatized by peers, administrators, alumni, and faculty.[57] Perhaps most detrimentally, professors may hold more negative attitudes toward them than anyone else on campus. Thus, they regularly encounter low expectations in classrooms where professors are skeptical of their academic abilities and don't challenge them to excel academically the way their coaches do athletically.[58] Because these young women and men are rarely provided with the framework that will allow them to successfully achieve both, their academic potential often goes untapped. This is particularly troubling, as positive and encouraging interactions with faculty are especially critical for this population's academic success.[59] Any radical reform of college sport must address this barrier. Fortunately, as we discuss in chapter 4, the overall increase in graduation rates shows progress can be made with intentional focus and additional resources.

Transition Outcomes

Fewer than 2% of all college men's basketball and football players will play at the professional level.[60] This means that the other 98% of student-athletes need to be prepared to get and perform jobs outside of their respective field of play. Participation in intercollegiate athletics is touted as a priceless opportunity to procure an education and a job. However, surprisingly little is known about the ways in which this participation ultimately impacts students' ability to actualize career aspirations. The scant research available suggests Division I student-athletes are most likely to experience unhealthy transitions out of sports. A 2007 study found that as they ended their sport careers and adjusted to post-sport life, revenue-athletes reported career transition difficulties and negative emotions, from feelings of loss and identity crises to distress.[61] While their nonsport peers utilize the professional services available on campus more than they do, college athletes endure a host of psychological and mental health–related issues as much as or more than their peers, such as fear of success, identity conflict, social isolation, and career anxiety.[62] Assessments of collegiate male athletes' life satisfaction at the termination of their collegiate careers indicated that Black athletes and students who did not have postcollege employment plans were significantly less satisfied with life.[63] Those with the strongest athletic identities at the time of sport retirement experience the greatest loss of identity[64] and need more time to adjust to life without it.[65] A function of the prioritization of athletic over academic and professional development is that some revenue-athletes depart from college less developed and prepared for life than when they entered.

Conclusion

This is the scene that is performed on the collegiate sports stage. This is the data that points to the most problematic academic outcomes for athletes who were, at some point in their lives, at least, projected to make it to the pros. The paths that need to be carved more clearly are for the success of the athletes who do not reach their professional goals—a reentry moment for those who fail to play professionally as well as those who do, with the idea of assisting both groups in attaining a meaningful degree. These initiatives, of course, would couple efforts to ensure academic success while student-athletes are still playing out their careers.

The story of Kevin Ross that opened this chapter is, fortunately, a tale of days gone by, but also a reminder of how negative life can become for the individual who puts all his eggs in the athletic basket while operating within a system that provides insufficient safeguards.

The next chapter looks at the previous attempts at student-athlete compensation reform, including the one-sided Ivy and professional models, and explains why they haven't gained much traction. It concludes by proposing that, rather than severing athletics and academics, we should frame the compensation discourse around ensuring that student-athletes reap all of college's benefits.

Chapter 3

Time for Change?

There's got to be a better way to balance the time intensity. Things have gotten so much worse in terms of the hours a week that it takes. I don't know if the answer is cutting back on the hours or what, but we need something that allows guys to study what they're really interested in and helps them with their education. Just policies that actually go along with education would be stuff to change.[66]

Kain Colter's education differs vastly from that of Kevin Ross. Colter is best known as one of the leaders of the college sport unionization movement, discussed in chapter 5, that emanated out of Northwestern University. His sport was football, and he came to Northwestern in 2010 with aspirations to be a doctor. But in the end, and largely because of his on-the-field obligations to football, he pursued a psychology degree instead of premed. He did well, earning a 3.0 grade point average (GPA), but he had his regrets; after all, he had wanted to be an orthopedic surgeon. "It makes it hard for you to succeed, you can't ever reach your academic potential with the time demands. You have to sacrifice, and we're not allowed to sacrifice football," Colter told the *New York Times*.[67] What's particularly striking is that Colter was attending one of the institutions that critics typically point to as being one of the few that properly balances big-time sports with big-time academics. Colter's reality, however, amplifies what the reader should accept as a recurring mantra: Achieving success in both academics and athletics is very difficult for anyone, regardless of desire, ability, or institution.

Chapter 1 explained how lucrative the enterprise of college sports has become. Chapter 2 acknowledged the steadily rising graduation rates seen among college athletes, while calling attention to some of the gaping educational holes that remain. Here in chapter 3 we simply propose that the ballooning revenue in college sports should be leveraged to provide student-athletes with the best education money can buy.

We know from the earlier chapters that the discussions regarding reforming college sports are not new. We also know that the focus has evolved over the years, from amateurism, to safety, to the elimination of scandal, to academic eligibility, to today's focus on the distribution of revenues. The tenor of the conversations has, as one might expect, evolved since the 1800s. We now aim to shift the discourse to meaningful degree completion.

Let us reflect for a moment on where college sport is now. While doing so, it's important to be aware that many in the system, including Ohio State University president Michael Drake, make statements indicating that they are largely fine with the status quo. Drake noted recently that providing the traditional package of room, board, tuition, and educational fees has been "overwhelmingly successful in helping people get an education and go on and do great things in their lives."[68] Drake is not alone in this viewpoint. He observed that his "father was a student-athlete many years ago."[69] This is an example of the institutional inertia that any new initiative to reform college sport must move against. The current model, broken or not, has served many well for many years; of this there is actually no debate. As was noted in the preface, Ken, one of the authors, was essentially fine with the current state of affairs, too, thinking that the student-athlete could be successful if he or she worked hard enough—that is, until he took a closer look at the reality. This is no longer your father's college sports system.

After briefly chronicling the history of student-athlete compensation, we describe the current model and a variety of proposed solutions. We conclude by detailing why it is in the best interest of both the institutions (NCAA, colleges and universities, and conferences) and the individual (student-athletes) to invest more deeply in academics, and explain how all parties can succeed if they are provided the right framework (detailed in chapter 4). Above all, it will take narrative-shifting culture change for us to reimagine the amateurism and student-athlete ideals.

Student-Athlete Compensation over the Years

Though the amateur and student-athlete ideals operate under the espoused goals of playing merely "for the love of the game" and valuing education over economic gain, the truth is that college athletes have always been, to some extent, paid. From the professional boatman *hired* and disguised as a Harvard student in the very first intercollegiate contest in 1852[70] to the 81 of 112 schools surveyed and exposed in the Carnegie report for recruiting and paying athletes in a variety of prohibited ways, compensation in the early years ranged from under-the-counter payments via disguised booster funds to no-show jobs and illegal scholarships called "subsidies."[71] The national debate over whether college athletes should be paid, first launched by the Carnegie Foundation report in 1929, reemerged in 1939 when first-year athletes at the University of Pittsburgh went on strike because their older teammates earned bigger paychecks.

College sport was so heavily shrouded in bribery and gambling scandals by 1946 that the NCAA deemed it necessary to compromise and reward college athletes for their sporting contributions.[72] Enacted in 1948, the Sanity Code allowed colleges and universities to compensate athletes via scholarships so long as they did not exceed the cost of tuition and meals.[73] Though seemingly fair and somewhat necessary, allowing financial aid to be awarded on the basis of athletic ability set a momentous and, perhaps dangerous, precedent.

First, this meant the version of amateurism adopted from British aristocracy was officially a thing of the past. In its original, exclusionary form, amateurism's primary intent was to snuff out any sign of professionalism and prevent lower-class athletes from joining the ranks of society's elite scholars. Then the NCAA itself incorporated professionalism into its constitution and bylaws, all the while positioning itself as upholder of the amateur ideal. This legislation signified the shifting of priorities. In contrast to the many instances of major actors in collegiate sport succumbing to the commercial pressure of sport, the NCAA had never been the perpetrator. With the decision to reward student-athletes according to their sporting ability, the organization had, and so the message was clear: Competitive college sports were a major priority. To be clear, we are avid supporters of scholarships. We just believe they are in need of a comprehensive revamping, rather than piecemeal add-ons.

Since establishing tuition and meals as the value of an athlete's commitment, the NCAA has diligently sought to maintain the athletic scholarship as the maximum compensation, a salary cap of sorts. The term "student-athlete," for example, was a calculated legal defense to safeguard the NCAA from any major workmen's compensation or death benefits payouts for athletes injured playing football. By placing "student" in front of "athlete" in all of its documents, the NCAA promoted the amateur ideal of academics over athletics, emphasized players' status as students, and prevented them from being identified as employees.

In the decades since, the skyrocketing revenues have prompted questions about what athletes are getting in return academically and financially. At every turn, college sport grows more profitable, and yet what student-athletes are given for creating this multibillion-dollar enterprise remains relatively stagnant. Comprehensive insurance coverage and injury protection, for example, are still on the to-do list. Accordingly, the perception of an uneven exchange between what athletes give and what they receive (exploitation) has led to unionization attempts and antitrust lawsuits by both current and former players.

Models

Much of the discussion on reform in college sports focuses on an all-or-nothing restructuring. That is, college sport in America goes to either the Ivy League model, with no athletic scholarships, or an open market, with schools bidding for the services of athletes on the traditional capitalist model. Though both are feasible, neither is ideal. An Ivy model will eliminate scholarships for many and limit access to higher education for some. It also reduces the potential for focused, high-level athletic competition and professional sport outcomes. The open market, by contrast, perhaps inevitably comes at the expense of any serious focus on degree completion and academic success. The structure of each of these models is explained in more detail in the following section.

The Ivy League Model: No Athletic Scholarships

We could simply assert, as some do, that college sports would be better off if we were to eliminate athletic scholarships completely. The absence of athletic scholarships and other financial incentives would mean all students would be selected and evaluated for admission primarily for their academic talents and successes. In turn, proponents say, this would lead to a dramatic decline in academic fraud and related athletic scandals. For those who aspire to the mythical "amateur" system, the Ivy model symbolizes a purer version of college sport. The authors of this book, both of whom have spent time with the Ivy model at the University of Pennsylvania, can attest that this kind of collegiate sports presence can provide an extraordinarily valuable atmosphere.

Perhaps the Ivy model's most salient feature is the embodiment of the student-athlete ideal. In this setting, athletes spend an extraordinary amount of time on sport, and in some instances, away from study. But they are also able to take part in campus life more fully than their peers at Power 5 universities. In many instances, their contributions in the classroom and in other extracurricular activities surpass their achievements on the field or court. They are often community leaders, honor society members, renowned performance artists, and model citizens integrated in the very fiber of student life.

Take Dau Jok, for example, a student-athlete at Penn during both of our tenures, who after fleeing from war-torn Sudan[74] created a foundation to educate Sudanese youth through sports. His legacy will be built much more around the volunteer and humanitarian work he's done serving international communities than it will be for serving as a captain of the men's basketball team.

In the Ivy model, multitalented students are commonplace. It can be argued, as many do, that their participation in sport enhances rather than hinders these athletes' personal, academic, and professional growth and development. What the Ivy model shows us is that the lofty ideal of the student-athlete is achievable. In fact, not only is it achievable but also it exists—and endures—even without the promise of financial benefit.

So what's missing? Well, quite obviously, access for students based on their athletic ability. It is certainly the case that if a given student-athlete is good enough to play in the big time, he will probably have the athletic scholarship option to attend elsewhere. And who could blame him? Athletic scholarships present a unique opportunity for students who might not otherwise have the means to attend a four-year college or university. Considering the inequities in the American education system, the barriers to enrolling in college are many and further exacerbated for people of color and those from low-income and first-generation college households. As we discuss in detail later in this chapter, using sport as a way to access the benefits of a higher education is a feature we desperately want to maintain.

Professionalization: Separate from Education

Years of scholarly research suggests that ethical compromises and corruption are endemic in institutions where big-time sports are present. As a result, more models completely separating academics and athletics are being offered and considered. Though more prominent as of late, this approach isn't exactly new, especially on a global scale. Noted earlier, the United States is the only country that develops the majority of its elite athletic talent on college and university campuses. Elsewhere in the world, serious athletes compete in local clubs and leagues completely removed from scholastic pursuits.[75] So the question essentially becomes, as that Carnegie report of so many years ago asked, what do competitive sports have to do with the institutions of higher learning? The answer may be nothing at all. But having been so closely connected to higher learning[76] since their inception, it is difficult to even imagine what a formal separation for college athletics would look like. Frankly, we remain uncertain about how this could work.

One proposed version of this fair-market model suggests that football and men's basketball teams become "professional" franchises owned and operated by the university, with student-athletes officially serving as employees. Instead of scholarships, high-profile athletes would earn salaries based on their individual market values, completely free from NCAA jurisdiction. With serious implications for the role and profitability of the NCAA, this and other proposed solutions have been met with scrutiny and gained little traction. Those conversations, we believe, also distract institutions from how they can best achieve their educational missions.

The further you move away from trying to make a sustainable, commonsense connection between academics and athletics, the closer you get to just creating another professional league. That certainly is an option. We offer no commentary here on the need for a new league in an already crowded American sports landscape, although absent affiliation with one of the existing big four sports leagues in the United States, success seems highly unlikely. Of greater concern than the feasibility of a new league is what is at stake if we were to completely sever the ties between academics and athletics.

While the Ivy model removes tuition, room, and board as standardized compensation for athletic participation, the professionalization model asserts that college and competitive sport are intrinsically conflicting endeavors and have no business cohabitating in the postsecondary environment. Wary of the ways in which the Ivy model limits college access for students from atypical backgrounds, the professionalization model even more severely separates a class of students from higher education. This also leads us to the disproportionate impact on a specific segment of the population, due to their overrepresentation in college basketball and football. The largest demographic of student-athletes that compete in the most popular and lucrative athletics programs is Black men. At the 65 Power 5 conference schools that routinely compete for championships, Black men represent 56.3% of football rosters and 60.8% of men's basketball rosters, but only 2.5% of all undergraduates on campus.[77] Were we to separate competitive sport from education, it is very likely that these men would be the most populous group in the hypothetical new "professional" league. The correlation, then, is clear: Removing competitive sports from campus would also remove a significant percentage of the Black men on those campuses. Because these individuals often come from communities where they are already socialized to believe that sports are the only "way out," separation of school and sport would further perpetuate this problematic notion. Again, we understand that life can be fine, and even exceptional, without a college degree. The data shows, however, that those who hold college degrees are more likely to be successful, to be happy, and able to positively impact society.[78] As we noted at the outset, while sport pays for a select few, education pays for most.

Hybrid Models

As high-profile college sports grow more commercialized and increasingly profitable, new models of intercollegiate athletics need to be developed.

The Olympic Model

One proposed solution resembles the Olympic model, which would maintain the current academic expectations of being a full-time student but would also allow the athletes on revenue-generating teams to profit beyond tuition, room, and board. High-profile athletes would be able to earn extra income from endorsements, appearances, and autograph signings, and could receive additional stipends based on their fair market value. It remains to be seen how the endorsement market would react to this, and whether it would actually benefit many student-athletes. After all, fewer athletes have endorsements, even at the professional level, than people tend to believe.

Conference-Athlete Revenue-Sharing Model

Another potential model, the conference-athlete revenue sharing model, seeks to propose a middle ground in a way that preserves both the virtues of the current system and the NCAA. In this system, outside of revenue sports, amateurism would continue as is; however, a conference-based, rather than college-based, revenue-sharing model would be implemented. This model makes the Power 5 conferences responsible for negotiating a revenue-sharing model that improves athlete welfare, saves the status quo, and reduces excess. Presumably a trade association or labor union would be formed by the student-athletes to serve as the counterpart to conference "management" in this collective bargaining scenario.[79]

While both of these models address compensation, they pay little attention to education. Thus, we provide another proposal as an alternative.

Meaningful Degree Model

Recognizing the tenuous relationship between school and sport, the model we propose—the Meaningful Degree Model—separates revenue sports from nonrevenue sports to create a Super Division with its own set of regulations. While the nonrevenue sports would proceed under the current model, the Power 5 "division" would operate as a separate entity. There, athletes would be granted "lifetime scholarships" that would allow them the flexibility to either pursue their undergraduate degree as a traditional full-time student, take a reduced academic course load during the season, extend the window of time with which to graduate, or have infinite access to their scholarship. This would afford participants the opportunity to pursue professional aspirations and return to school after they transition out of sports. This model uses counseling to custom tailor each individual student-athlete's path to success.

Title IX equivalencies would need to be provided throughout the system. The important issues of equal opportunities and funding for female athletes are, in our minds, a no-compromise complexity in any reform model. Compliance with existing laws is simply another part of this complex reform puzzle.

Seriousness would also dictate beginning with academic "boot camps" to introduce students to the type and intensity of college-level work as well as customizing opportunities for student-athletes to engage in educationally purposeful activities, including extracurricular groups, study abroad, and internships. Similar efforts currently take place at many institutions for nonathlete students, including some highly selective institutions.

In some sense, this is where we are today, as much of this conversation is already taking place with regard to the Power 5 conferences. However, our conception of a Super Division preserves the amateur ideal by only temporarily professionalizing the elite athletes within it. By expanding the depth and breadth of the athletic scholarship to a "lifetime scholarship," we seek to wed athletic aspiration not just to college access and opportunity but to college completion, success, and the actualization of postgraduate benefits. How this is accomplished is detailed in chapter 4.

Realism and Reform: Why Both Athletics and Academics Are Important

It is this course that brings us to the most difficult outcome: Do both. Our contention is that these young men and women have a long life ahead of them. Even if they have a career in professional sports, the reality is that it will not last forever (in fact, the National Football League [NFL] goes to great lengths to make incoming rookies understand that football is not a "career" but rather an "experience"—one that often lasts only a few short seasons). It is a common statement that athletes die two deaths, the first one being when they, voluntarily or not, retire.

Most of us have time to make a decision about what we will do with our lives, and will follow a more linear path toward that goal, with the usual ups and downs along the way. The athlete, by contrast, takes a unique path. It begins with a focus solely on athletic success. Alternative careers may not even be contemplated. Disturbingly too, as Kain Colter's testimony in the Northwestern unionization case displayed for us, if the initial academic dreams are not feasible to complete due to practice and other schedule restrictions, one dream or another may in reality be untenable.

The second career path for the athlete is far from linear. For many athletes, even finding this career trail is challenging given their limited exposure to assets and programs more readily available to other students. The degree program is just one aspect of this path forward; the other is engagement in activities that will allow this life after sport reflection to occur. Recognizing this unique athletic trajectory, we propose structuring lifetime scholarships in such a way so as to allow athletes to initially focus on sport and return to school after their playing days are over. Why? Because in a debate about student-athlete compensation, few recognize that education pays most.

Education Pays for Individuals

National reports have revealed myriad benefits of a college education for both individuals and society. College graduates are not only more likely to be employed than high school graduates, but also more likely to find better jobs, earn more money, and have health insurance and pension benefits provided by their employers. They also commit fewer crimes, live longer and healthier lives, and contribute to society as productive and civically engaged citizens. On virtually every measure of economic and career success, young college graduates out-perform their less educated peers.[80] In short, education pays.

Economics aside, substantial evidence indicates that college completion, not just individual skills and knowledge, is strongly associated with healthier lifestyles, active citizenship, and increased educational activities and opportunities for graduates' children. Since information about smoking risks has become public, for instance, college graduates have smoked at rates significantly lower than those of other adults. They are also more likely to exercise and less likely to be obese. This also holds true for their children, who are more likely to be breast-fed and less likely to be low-birth-weight babies. The college-educated display active citizenship by their propensity to donate, volunteer, and vote. Finally, these individuals' children engage in more educational activities and are, in general, better pre-pared for school. Unsurprisingly, college graduates are significantly more likely than high school graduates to report being very happy.

Education Can Pay for the NCAA and Member Institutions

The lifetime scholarship also presents an opportunity for the NCAA to (1) improve the student-athlete experience, (2) reorient the dis-course around education, (3) continue to operate as an amateur enter-prise, (4) maintain the status quo by sustaining its revenue model, and (5) position itself on the right side of the college athletic reform debate.

The defining characteristic of the student-athlete experience is the lack of time. While athletic scholarships provide the opportunity for student-athletes to access the college environment, the time com-mitment and physical demands of sport at the most competitive levels make it difficult to achieve anywhere but on the field of play. By giving athletes the freedom to first fully commit to sport and then fully commit to academic and professional development, the lifetime scholarship model removes the greatest threat to student-athlete success: the college "shot clock." Absent limits on the time it takes to complete their degree, adequate attention can be paid to coursework, study abroad, internships, and other academically purposeful activities that lead to improved postcollege and employment outcomes. Thus, this approach can intertwine the academic mission of universities and athletes' goals of greater economic opportunity.

Reorienting the compensation reform discourse around academic success and employment outcomes reiterates the presence and significance of the amateurism and student-athlete ideals. As much of the criticism of the NCAA results from its prioritization of athletics over academics, student success-centered legislation reaffirms what the NCAA represents and why its regulation is needed. Moreover, the sooner the NCAA speaks up, the better. Often seeming reactionary versus proactive in its response to calls for reform, the NCAA can show that it is serious about its academic principles by implementing change before it is mandated.

The next chapter explains how to best use increased revenues to benefit student-athletes. It lays out programs for athletes prior to their arrival on campus, during their time there, and after they leave. The proposed programs range from preparatory and tutorial programs to funds for the return to college following their attempts at professional sports careers.

Chapter 4

The Solution: Constructive, Disruptive Systemic Change

You plan your day, your meals, and your study time around it. Everything is based on when I have practice next, what workout I have to be at, what is this going to do for my image as a football player, what kind of things am I going to be participating in, and how is it going to affect me as a football player. It's always football first, everything else is secondary. Friends can wait. Everything else can wait. You have your whole life to finish school, but you only get five years of eligibility.[81]

R egularly ranked among the top five public universities in the United States by *U.S. News and World Report*[82] for its selective admissions, progressive financial-aid policies, and groundbreaking research, the University of North Carolina at Chapel Hill is also the home of one of the nation's most storied basketball programs. The alma mater of Michael Jordan, arguably the greatest basketball player of all time, North Carolina boasts 20 Final Four appearances, 49 Atlantic Coast Conference championships, and 6 NCAA men's basketball championships, the most recent in 2017.

However, since the 2014 season, the school has been under investigation for what Fox Sports has dubbed the "most egregious academic fraud scandal in NCAA history."[83] Once touted as a pantheon of academic and athletic success, Chapel Hill has had its reputation muddied by an 18-year scandal in which students (predominantly student-athletes) were allegedly enrolled in fake "paper classes" in

African- and Afro-American studies to boost their GPAs. Between 1993 and 2011, it is alleged that more than 3,100 students used those courses to maintain their eligibility and graduate.

The reality in sport is that there is always, unfortunately, someone or some enterprise willing to cheat. We do not delude ourselves in thinking that we could ever develop a system that would guarantee that the educational interest of student-athletes would always come first. From Deflategate in the NFL, to the junior tennis player lying about a line call, to performance-enhancing drugs across all sports, the willingness to violate rules for greater success seems to be never ending, and is very likely inevitable. So, we move with caution as we explore some changes that might make the situation better, understanding that there is in fact no ultimate panacea.

Chapter 4 explains how the model can best use increased revenues to benefit student-athletes. The chapter begins by exploring the relationship between sport, education, and opportunity. It then details the Student-Athlete Manifesto, laying out programs for athletes prior to their arrival on campus, during their time there, and after they leave their respective institutions, from preparatory and tutorial programs to funds for the return to college after their attempts at professional careers. We conclude on a cautionary note, addressing the need for academic oversight and external accountability.

Sport, Education, and Opportunity

The student-athlete compensation reform debate is bigger than sports. Since the 1946 Sanity Code legislation allowing athletes to access higher education in exchange for their athletic talents, competitive college sports have become an additional avenue through which the American Dream can be pursued. Of the 16% of student-athletes who reported being first-generation college students (defined as neither parent having attended college), less than half of them strongly agreed they would have attended a four-year college had they not been an athlete.[84] Thus, for people whose parents did not go to college, the athletic scholarship presents an opportunity for them to pull themselves up by their bootstraps, or in this case, gym shoe laces.

Though athletic scholarships provide an opportunity for student-athletes to access the college environment, the time commitment and physical demands of sport at the most competitive levels make it difficult to achieve academically. As few will go on to live fruitful lives as professional athletes, it is imperative that student-athletes spend an adequate amount of time on coursework, study abroad, internships, and other academically purposeful activities that lead to improved postcollege and employment outcomes. However, the current system affords student-athletes little time to be both serious students and athletes, thus inherently putting athletics and academics in direct competition with each other. This fundamental shortcoming, we contend, is why the college sports model is in need of systemic change—defined as change that pervades all parts of a system and accounts for the relationships among them. This systemic change must be primarily focused on eradicating educational inequities.

Equity versus Equality

We mentioned equity at the beginning of this book as our ultimate goal—equity for all student-athletes. The Meaningful Degree Model is grounded in this notion. Though often used interchangeably, equity and equality are quite different. *Equality* simply means sameness. Regardless of need or any other individual difference, everyone is treated the same exact way. *Equity*, on the other hand, means fairness. It is the process by which everyone is provided with what they need to succeed. Whereas equality is the goal, equity is the system by which we achieve it. In an equality model, a coach gives all of his players the exact same shoes in the same exact size. In an equity model, the coach gives all of his players the same shoes, but in their size.

In college sports, education, and elsewhere in American society, our preoccupation with treating everyone the same irrespective of race, sex, caste, creed, nationality, disability, age, religion, sexual orientation, gender identity, and so on, has distracted us from the fact that all people are *not* created equal. If everyone were the same, equal treatment would be fair and ensure equal outcomes for all. However, because that is not the case, treating everyone the same allows disparities to persist. Recognizing that the starting point of individuals in American society has never been and may never be the same, to reach the goal of equality, we must treat people equitably, or in a way that recognizes their individual needs and circumstances.

Again, while equality means everyone gets the same, equity means everyone gets what they need to succeed.

Prep for Prep: A Model of Educational Equity

We convey this grander path toward equity because it all begins well before these men and women reach college. Sometimes it is hard to identify. At Wynandotte High School in Kansas City, Kevin Ross, whom we introduced you to in chapter 2, had a 2.0 GPA. At Creighton University, he had a reported 0.54. What mattered most as he entered Creighton, however, was not how well or how poorly he was doing in school, but rather that he was averaging 20 points and 20 rebounds per game, making him a coveted recruit—and a future star. Sadly, neither basketball nor grades were good for him at Creighton. There he averaged only 4.2 points per game, and his academic situation only grew worse.[85] One piece of the puzzle in how such a situation might be prevented is a program called Prep for Prep.

Prep for Prep (preparation for prep school) is a New York City–based nonprofit that offers promising low-income students of color access to a private school education via academic, as opposed to athletic, scholarships.[86] We highlight this program, also referred to as just "Prep," because its equity model systemically changes participants' lives. Accordingly, the leadership development program considers the whole student, preemptively accounting for potential barriers to success and exposing participants to a variety of enriching experiences and opportunities to mitigate them. Prep not only incorporates a rigorous 14-month academic component to prepare students for placement in leading independent schools, but also continues to work closely with the students through high school graduation, the college process, and beyond.

Low-income students of color transitioning from large public schools to small, affluent, predominantly white private schools will undoubtedly face culture shock. Prep prepares them for both the academic rigor and the racial, ethnic, and socioeconomic challenges they may encounter. The preparatory component begins with two extensive sessions of summer school after fifth grade and sixth grade, and after-school and Saturday sessions during sixth grade. In addition to courses that include history, literature, English, math, writing skills, Spanish or French, Latin, physical education, research skills, and science, an experiential course titled Invictus explores issues of diversity in the United States to make students aware of and equipped for these sociocultural challenges.

Additionally, Prep offers a range of services to help students adjust academically and socially to their new schools. For example, the program's staff plans weekly social events for recent graduates to come together and cultivate relationships with students who come from backgrounds similar to their own. The Leadership Development Component features a mandatory series of retreats known as Aspects of Leadership, which include modules on ethics, community roles and responsibilities, and leadership. Optional activities include study abroad programs and domestic cultural opportunities, as well as career panels, résumé writing seminars, interviewing workshops, and prized internships.

In the college preparatory component, the program assists students with the college search, application, and choice processes. Participants are afforded private sessions where they learn about schools, take trips to college campuses and meet one-on-one with admissions officers, and spend time with advisers who assist them with identifying need-based scholarships, filling out financial aid forms, and perfecting their applications. Once they enroll in college,

Prep students remain connected to the program and their peers through college counselors, the College Summer Jobs Bank, and other professional and social networking opportunities. Prep's college counselors even travel to students' colleges and universities to ensure that their first-year transitions are smooth and that they are well acquainted with campus resources.

For Prep alums, the professional development opportunities extend even after college. The program leverages its existing relationships to provide an extensive network for college graduates seeking employment or career transition assistance. The work is not done until Prep students are paid, not directly by the program itself, but by the top employers seeking the next generation of the country's diverse talent.

In the education literature, the Prep for Prep journey can be defined as academic capital formation.[87] It is a social process that builds knowledge of educational and career options and supports navigation through educational and professional systems. These particular interventions, programs, and services can equip students from low-income backgrounds (and their families) with knowledge of and membership in networks that ultimately help them access colleges and universities, attain postsecondary degrees, and transition into the middle class.[88] With the Prep model in mind, the question then is, what do equity and academic capital formation look like in college sports?

Equity in College Sports

An equity model for college sports sets college completion and employment as the goals, and then works backward to provide the tools and resources needed for all student-athletes to achieve them. Equity would entail making sure that each person enrolled not only graduated but graduated having had a diverse set of experiences that prepared them for a career and life after college. By customizing a process that graduates and focuses on future employment for all the student-athletes, the proposed model aims to provide this outcome for all who enter collegiate sport as scholarship athletes. This demographic includes low-income students, first-generation college students, and students of color who are overrepresented on Power 5 conference men's basketball and football teams. Often, these student-athletes attended less challenging high schools, performed worse on standardized tests, and were recruited and enrolled despite being less prepared than their nonsport peers. The Student-Athlete Manifesto that follows outlines steps to achieve success for all student-athletes by accounting for the most vulnerable among them.

The Student-Athlete Manifesto

The Student-Athlete Manifesto seeks to:

1) Make obtaining a *meaningful* degree the priority—*not* football, basketball, or any sport.

In his dissertation on student-athletes' assessments of their collegiate experiences, Collin, one of the authors, found that participation in Division I sports is driven more by opportunity than it is by academics or by love of the game. For many, sports ceased to be just a hobby in high school. While recruited athletes aspire to play professionally because of the financial freedom it may eventually afford their families, walk-ons played with hopes of alleviating the burden of college cost on their families and themselves. Regardless of their root motivations, however, athletes at Power 5 schools explained that coaches, staff, and other administrators made it clear from the beginning that

> in the FBS [Football Bowl Subdivision], it's definitely football first and school second. Either directly or indirectly, they let you know how important football is. If you're not going to give a 100 percent in your commitment to the sport, your development as a player, your investment in the team, and your teammates, then you don't belong there. It's made clear to you. The environment makes that known by being a part of it.[89]

In many instances, coaches outwardly told players that they had to choose between the three worlds of sports, academics, and a social life. There is not enough time for two, much less all three. With the time limitations on athletic eligibility and the narrow age windows with which one can realistically enter professional sports, we acknowledge that sports success is, to some extent, more urgent. However, we also recognize that this urgency is in direct competition with the quality of the *free* education they are supposed to be simultaneously receiving. For this reason, we suggest that school and sport be staggered, so even the most challenging and time-consuming courses of study can be pursued after playing. In return for student-athletes' commitment to sport on the front end, the university commits to their academic and professional development on the back end. This approach shifts the discussion from *either* student or athlete to *both* student and athlete.

2) Broaden the pathway to meaningful degree completion by granting athletes the right to return to complete the degree, including one-and-done athletes.

The lifetime scholarship is the key feature of the manifesto. Discussed throughout, the single biggest impediment to the revenue-athlete experience is the lack of time to dedicate to both sports and school. By extending the time allotted to complete their degree, the lifetime scholarship allows student-athletes to choose how they want to spread out their academic course load. While those exceptional at multitasking will have the option of balancing their academics and athletics at the same time, athletes that require it will have more time to get where they need to be academically without being rushed. In fact, this additional time affords them the opportunity to enrich the college experience however the student-athlete and their adviser see fit. Primarily, this addresses the pervasive problem of achieving the *desired* degree, allowing athletes to major in the subject of their choice, spend time building relationships with professors, interact with other students in said major, and utilize tutoring and other resources.

With the lifetime scholarship, for example, a starting quarterback like Northwestern University's Kain Colter would not have been forced to change his career aspirations away from being an orthopedic surgeon simply because science courses conflicted with football practice schedules. His timeline in completing the degree, however, may have been altered. Five years may not have been enough time, but coming back at a later date, calculated via counseling on entry, is wholly feasible.

Variations of the lifetime scholarship that we propose have been announced and recommended in years past. As NCAA rules allow scholarships to be pulled or reduced each year, some institutions have eased these concerns and demonstrated a commitment to degree completion by guaranteeing their student-athletes' tuition, room, and board for all four years. A smaller set of schools have gone further and extended the scholarship guarantee beyond the expiration of one's eligibility. The University of Kentucky's Post-Eligibility Program, launched in 1989, pays for tuition and books for former athletes who left to pursue professional sport careers but then returned to school, with no restriction on time. For example, inspired by both of his sons earning degrees, Oliver White, a former University of Kentucky football player, returned to campus 30 years after leaving a semester early for the NFL draft to complete his own degree.[90] Introduced in 2014 at the University of Maryland, the Maryland Way Guarantee allows student-athletes across all sports, not just the revenue-generating sports of basketball and football, to return and pursue completing their degree after their eligibility has expired.[91] Pioneers in these endeavors, these schools' athletics directors were dedicated to college sports being first and foremost about education and preparing students to serve as leaders in local, state, and global communities.

Though a commendable step forward, these initiatives fail to provide the educational extension needed for those who want to pursue degrees that include classwork that conflicts with practices and other responsibilities while they are on campus. For this idea to work, however, greater reform of the rules would need to be implemented.

Flexibility would be essential as we worked to provide opportunities for student-athletes to attain their highest academic potential, or at least forge a path that aligns with their aspirations. What we don't want is to find ourselves at a point where student-athletes are taking courses that ultimately do not lead to a meaningful degree. If an athlete has no sincere interest in a serious academic program, maybe a purely professional path as an athlete is the right way forward. Here, we would need to explore further a model for these athletes in which academics is not at all part of the venture, or is limited in such a way that engages athletes in some form of study but does not clash with their stated desire to focus on sports first. We are not recommending that here; we are merely acknowledging that it may need to be addressed.

The lifetime scholarship also affords more time for personal and professional development, lessening the likelihood of unhealthy transitions out of sport. Whether still on campus or returning after their professional sport pursuits, athletes also have the opportunity to engage in other facets of student life, from student government and fraternity and sorority life to performance arts groups, research, and study abroad.

Once I didn't make it, and I was no longer able to play football, I kind of hit a wall. I had to discover who I was and what I'm into. I'm still in that process. I think that if I had gone to college, and I hadn't played a sport, I would. Others joined a fraternity, started teaching on campus, and just did different things. You developed an identity, several identities. My identity has always been . . . I've always been a football player. Once that's taken away, it's kind of like, "Now what?"[92]

Identity-related issues, dependence on formalized structures, and relatively rougher transitions out of college than those of their non-athlete peers are among the developmental costs of competitive college athletics. After having all the structure, organization, and "free" stuff given to them because of their athletic ability, revenue-athletes have to adapt to a whole new environment where everything is on them. All of a sudden, they are thrown into the real world, where things like taxes and health care and car insurance become real. Unsure if it was more because of the lack of time or the lack of preparation they received from the easier classes they took, revenue-generating athletes often feel less equipped to transition out of college than other students. The lifetime scholarship would expose them to the vast array of extracurricular activities on campus and provide both perspective into who these students are besides athletes and insight into what they want to do with their postcollege careers.

This academic success may require a reduced number of courses taken during the initial scholarship period—and we propose that this would be completely in alignment with our goal of ultimate academic success. As Seth Berger, a successful entrepreneur, high school basketball coach, and onetime college athlete wrote in *Sports Illustrated*, "These fixes alone won't solve all of the NCAA's problems, but they can help alleviate the pressure on athletes and coaches. These changes could go a long way toward helping the NCAA provide the best academic and athletic experiences for these young men and women who work so hard every day."[93]

3) Mandate academic boot camps for entering student-athletes and professional boot camps for exiting student-athletes.

The miseducation of student-athletes begins long before their arrival on campus. Middle and high schools, as well as families and communities, disproportionately focus on students' athletic prowess and then often pass them along to the universities that recruit them despite the fact that they may be woefully unprepared for the rigors of college-level work. Though institutions of higher education can't fix the pipeline issues overnight, they can be held responsible for educating all the students they enroll. Particularly effective methods for retaining and graduating students admitted below standard admissions criteria are precollege academic boot camps that increase student awareness of what will be expected of them scholastically. These initiatives give students not only a preview of the amount and extent of the work ahead but also an idea of their academic deficits and, importantly, time to identify the resources needed to close the gaps. Further, these boot camps allow students to test out courses without the fear of getting grades that can negatively affect their GPAs.

Preparatory boot camps can also mitigate some issues specific to student-athletes. Beyond coursework, this time may be used to introduce incoming players to the sociocultural challenges they may encounter. Like students in the Prep for Prep example, these students from low-income, first-generation college, and/or racial and ethnic minority backgrounds bring all of their identities with them to what may seem to be a whole new world. Precollege initiatives have been particularly effective for these vulnerable populations, as they are less likely to have had exposure to college outside of recruiting visits—visits during which schools paint perfect visions of campus life specifically to get them to attend.

Of particular concern are the "dumb jock" stereotype and imposter syndrome, which may impact student-athletes regardless of other background characteristics. Recognized more as athletes than as students by their peers and professors, student-athletes are often subject to low expectations in classrooms, not pushed to achieve academically, and not selected to do group work. A lack of familiarity and comfort with professors and sometimes even other students may result in limited interaction. As meaningful relationships with professors and nonsport peers lead to better academic outcomes, these boot camps can provide additional points of interaction, combating stereotypes on both sides. Leadership and diversity training from organizations such as RISE (Ross Initiative in Sports for Equality) provides customized curriculums to address these issues. Additional considerations are using the time before the season to start exploring potential majors, career interests, and extracurricular activities.

4) Make maximum use of summers for educational and professional development.

Of all the academically purposeful activities, none are of as much concern for top athletes as the internships, job shadows, and other types of professional development that they often miss out on because of their on-field responsibilities. These missed opportunities to explore potential career paths are damaging on multiple levels, because not only do their nonsport peers have more time to get better grades during the school year, they also have summers with which to gain work experience and tangible skills. Central to athletes' concerns about these professionally focused sacrifices is that they make them less competitive candidates in the future. As one former student-athlete reported, "Pretty much every single person that we've been competing with for jobs has had tons of work experience from their sophomore year on, while we have none. Literally, nothing."[94] The revenue-generating athletes reported feeling "behind the eight ball," because while athletic notoriety and fame might help get them in the door, they may never have acquired any of the technical and tangible workplace skills that their peers have. Additionally, while their stipends provided them "enough cash to get by," scholarship athletes do not have ways to earn extra cash for incidentals like transportation, food, and so on. Developmental summers directly address both of these concerns.

5) Expand the opportunity to get credits from institutions offering online opportunities.

In our work with the NFL's Player Engagement department, the division charged with assisting professional athletes' in their return to school and completion of their degrees, we have seen firsthand how logistical barriers can impede degree completion. Amid busy playing and practice schedules in 30-plus geographic locations, these men, despite their desire to succeed, struggle to find the time to return to campus when traditional courses are offered. For them and others, the expansion of the opportunity to enroll in courses, complete the work, and transfer credits from online courses back to their original institutions can facilitate them achieving their academic goals.

This is a particularly interesting proposition for female professional basketball players. They often play year-round in both the

Women's National Basketball Association and various leagues overseas. Their calendars make it extremely problematic, if not impossible, to contemplate degree completion in a traditional classroom setting.

6) Provide personalized counseling on the best paths among academic and career options.

As the college degree is by no means a cure-all, we believe there should be an evaluation of the various paths each individual can take. For some student-athletes, it's being encouraged to remain in a challenging major considering its long-term value. Others may be better served being redirected to trades or entrepreneurship instead of being steered into degree programs that would be of little value to complete. In each circumstance, it should be about what is most beneficial to the student, not what is most beneficial to the program. Each student-athlete ought to have an academic and career coach to counsel them on the best path to success, however it is defined for the individual. Pursue a different degree? Change her or his major and pursue additional courses to do so? Degree completion is not the ultimate solution. The focus must be on avoiding *miseducation* and earning *meaningful* degrees.

7) Review and enforce existing limits on hours of sports participation.

To minimize interference with the academic programs of its student-athletes,[95] the NCAA requires member institutions to limit their "countable athletically related activities," or sport-related activity involving student-athletes under the direction of the coaching staff.[96] During the season, student-athletes may not participate in countable athletically related activities for more than 4 hours per day and 20 hours per week. Despite these stated limitations, independent and NCAA studies regularly report that student-athletes spend upward of 40–50 hours per week on their sport. Absent extenuating circumstances such as being investigated for other infractions, the

20-hour rule receives varying levels of enforcement at member institutions.

In one interview, a student-athlete commented, "I don't think there is a 40-hour rule." In his experience, the in-season time commitment for football so regularly eclipsed the 40-hour mark that he had forgotten that the time restriction was actually 20 hours. Participants said they knew it was supposed to exist, but characterized the 20-hour rule as broken, not really paid attention to, and largely a joke. One reason why the number of hours greatly exceeds the time restrictions the NCAA put in place is the "optional," "voluntary," or "non-mandatory" activities that coaches expect players to organize and participate in without explicitly forcing them to.

> It's the obligations that aren't supposed to be mandatory. Like the meetings and the extra schedule of practices without the coaches or the lists of who is coming to get an extra lift . . . our coaches want you to go and do these things even though it's not mandatory, but if you don't show up, it reflects badly on you. Your chances of getting on the field drastically diminish. They always throw things back in your face like why didn't you come to this or why did you go to that. Even if you have homework and stuff like that, it's still looked at as you still should have made it. A lot of kids feel pushed or coerced to do things, extra things, for the team just to get out there and play.[97]

As so much rides on preparation for game day, limiting the hours spent on athletically related activities during the season may be the single hardest aspect of college sports to reform and enforce. Accordingly, then, the lifetime scholarship provides a framework in which coaches and players can dedicate the necessary time for sport without conflicting with academic endeavors. There is, however, more hope for how time is spent out of season.

This hour limitation is also problematic in delivering genuine counseling. The concern, as in so many areas, will come from competing institutions that the "counseling" is coaching and delivers a competitive advantage. This concern, and limitations on what is being delivered, must be overcome.

8) Enhance, but more closely monitor, tutoring support;

9) Make sure athletes are the ones actually doing the academic work; and

10) More stringently prohibit athlete-only or athlete-dominant courses.

In chapter 1, we detailed the ways the influx of revenue in college sport has led to the miseducation of the student-athlete. There is no need to repeat it here. In short, the commercial success of high-profile sports has regularly led to academic fraud as coaches, athletics directors, conference executives, and member institution officials have made ethical compromises to keep the top athletes eligible for competition. Thus, we contend that several measures need to be taken to maintain academic oversight. These include enhancing, and simultaneously more closely monitoring, tutoring support, making sure athletes are the ones actually doing their academic work (particularly for the online coursework), and more stringently prohibiting problematic athlete-dominant courses. Perhaps our most novel contribution here is the suggestion that the academic oversight come from an independent third party, such as an enhanced Knight Commission, or some other entity that could be funded either independently or via the revenues generated by big-time college sports. As academic integrity has proved to be a small price to pay for athletic excellence, it may be the case that only stakeholders who would not be consumed by competition are those not directly affected by it. In this sense, think of the growth of anti-doping agencies such as the US Anti-Doping Agency and the World Anti-Doping Agency, which exist solely for the purpose of monitoring performance-enhancing drug use.[98] A similar enterprise focused on collegiate sports could be impactful. If this is not an option, a rethinking of the focus of the enforcement wing of the NCAA would be the next best alternative.

11) Standardize a way to more accurately track all graduation rates;

12) Establish independently administered pre- and posttests to truly measure learning; and,

13) Increase accountability by requiring the NCAA to routinely report this data disaggregated by race, sex, sport, division, and particular subsets of institutions within a division (i.e., the Power 5 conferences).

Accountability is practically impossible without transparency. Accordingly, we propose three measures to achieve greater clarity on the impact of participation in sports on the student-athlete experience. The first is standardizing a metric to more accurately track all graduation rates. Currently, there exists no data with which we can directly compare the graduation rates of student-athletes and their nonsport peers. Because the federal graduation rate is imperfect, the NCAA created the graduation success rate (GSR) and the academic success rate (ASR), and while the federal graduation rate is believed to *underestimate* graduation numbers, the GSR and ASR are critiqued for *overestimating* them. Either way, this inconsistency of measures does not provide a clear picture of how student-athletes are performing relative to others. Thus, we contend a new standard measure that captures all students be created to facilitate these comparisons.

Second, we find it troubling that after more than three decades of focused research, higher-education researchers and college sport stakeholders have yet to produce an effective way of measuring "learning." That is, besides the imperfect graduation rates, relatively little is known about what else student-athletes (as well as other students) are actually learning in or taking away from college. It has been argued that even at the most selective universities, we know little about how much students really learn, as these schools get the elite academic talent and their later successes are often a result of the background characteristics they entered college with, or the network and brand of the institution. Though the entry requirements are high, there exists no exit measure to tell us the extent of the learning that took place. The only way for us to truly know the advances individuals make would be to administer a pretest and a posttest. This data, not just for sports but for higher education in general, would more accurately determine the way students have developed while in college.

Finally, we reiterate some of Harper's recommendations for improving equity in college sports.[99] College sport stakeholders should collect and disaggregate data by race, sex, sport, division, and particular subsets of institutions within a division (i.e., the Power 5 conferences). The NCAA, perhaps the Office of Inclusion, should establish a commission on equity that routinely calls for and responds to these disaggregated data reports, raises consciousness within and beyond the NCAA about the persistence and pervasiveness of inequities, and partners with athletic conferences and institutions to develop policies and programs that narrow performance gaps. Conferences should commit a portion of proceeds earned from championships and other revenue sources back to member institutions for programming and other interventions that aim to improve equity within and beyond sports. Campus leaders should pay more careful attention to differences in student-athletes' GPAs, classroom experiences, course enrollment and major selection patterns, and participation in enriching educational experiences beyond athletics. Athletics directors must collaborate with coaches and other staff in the department to devise a strategy for narrowing gaps in graduation rates, academic success indicators, and other student-athlete outcomes. Coaches must be involved in all phases of the process and view themselves as departmental agents who are rewarded for winning games and achieving equity in student-athlete success. Finally, athletics departments ought to create internal committees or task forces that focus on equity. This group should comprise stakeholders within and beyond the athletics department, including administrators from academic and student affairs, current and former student-athletes, and professors who study and write about race and/or sports.[100] Initially offered in 2013, these suggestions are worth revisiting.

The final chapter focuses on examples of success, the stakeholders that can push toward the elements of this manifesto, and some of the problems that may occur during implementation.

Chapter 5

Moving toward Change and Implementing Solutions

We have a governance structure that finally has the ability to take us there.[101]

—*Gene Smith, director of athletics, Ohio State University*

The year is 1988, and Kevin Ross is in the news again. He is far from a basketball court. Six years after he found himself sitting in the eighth-grade classroom of Marva Collins, where as a grown adult he was finally learning how to read, and a decade after he last took the floor at Creighton University, Ross now sits in a Quality Inn hotel room in Chicago, having thrown the contents of the eighth-story room out the window.[102] He is threatening to kill himself.

He has tried to get his life together. He has tried to overcome the shortcomings of his miseducation. But apparently in his mind he has failed. His academic and athletic failings continue to haunt him, and one would hope that his plight would serve as a wake-up call to the world of college sports.

Marva Collins is called on once again. Collins's words and 15 police officers subdue him, and he is taken to Cook County Hospital for observation. It is in this awful and, dare we say, preventable setting that Ross finally reveals his frustration at not being able to find a career a decade after leaving Creighton. In the end, fortunately, Collins and the police discovered Ross didn't have a gun; he was merely pushed to the edge, forced to confront his failed past—and perhaps those who failed him, too. The question, of course, is obvious:

How do we prevent student-athletes from experiencing this worst-case scenario?

To be fair, the situation in big-time college sports has improved quite a bit since the late 1980s. For instance, it is far less likely that someone in Kevin Ross's situation then could get that far through the system with the regulations and academic clearing houses that are in place today. Grades and assessment tests are now much more closely contemplated by authorities. It's almost staggering to think that level of suspect recruiting was even allowed to occur back then, in the relative dark days of college sport. But Ross's sad situation is an important reminder of where we once were—and where we must never return. Indeed, just think: When he was asked in a 2002 *Outside the Lines* interview if he could read when he enrolled at Creighton in 1978, Ross said, "I could read my name. Yes, I can read the name, and the school I went to."[103]

Today, classes like "The Theory of Basketball" and "Marksmanship" are no longer as readily available as they were in Ross's day, but equivalents exist. Further, the ongoing North Carolina saga, which includes serious allegations of sham courses, reveals to us that we must remain vigilant in the enforcement space, even when it comes to our most respected academic institutions. Although imperfect, the NCAA of today has successfully uncovered these behaviors and has been harsh in sanctioning them. We propose, however, that punishment is not enough. Reforms must be much more holistic.

Examples of Success

For all of the failures that we detail in this book, we also have seen over the years no shortage of positive outcomes from college sports. Well-known successes include Myron Rolle, a Rhodes Scholar who played at a high level for football powerhouse Florida State; Andrew Luck, who earned a degree in architectural engineering from Stanford and later emerged as the star quarterback for the Indianapolis Colts; and Malcolm Brogdon, who graduated with a master's degree from the University of Virginia and later won the 2017 NBA Rookie of the Year Award.

So, yes, *doing both is possible*. The key, though, is that each of these individuals was exceptional in being able to do both: to be an athlete and an accomplished student, and to be both within the traditional time frame afforded big-time college athletes. The reality we must face, of course, is that not all athletes can do this. Equity dictates that we take each athlete as she is and allow her to enter into a system that offers a path of success that will work for her.

Consider the following athletes, each of whom pursued a professional sports career only to return to school later and complete their degree. Marvin Williams, a one-and-done basketball player at North Carolina, was drafted second overall in the 2005 NBA Draft and left Chapel Hill with only a couple of credits under his belt. After returning to take classes each summer, often during both summer sessions, Marvin completed his degree in 2014, a full 10 years after he enrolled as a freshman. Similarly, a rising superstar by the name of Michael Jordan returned to Chapel Hill in 1986 to complete his degree in geography after being drafted in 1984. Vince Carter completed his coursework there in 2000 after being drafted in 1998. Shaquille O'Neal left Louisiana State University as a junior to go pro, and later completed his degree via distance learning. Impressively, he then continued on to get both his MBA and a PhD in education leadership. Venus Williams, after a dominating tennis career that began outside the collegiate system, earned her BS in business administration in 2015. Troy Polamalu, drafted in 2003 by the Pittsburgh Steelers, returned to the University of Southern California during the 2011 NFL lockout to complete a bachelor's degree in history. Elite NFL quarterback Ben Roethlisberger was drafted in 2004 and returned to complete his BS in education at Miami University of Ohio in 2012. Hall of Fame running back Emmitt Smith returned to the University of Florida to complete his degree in public recreation—and did so while still playing in the league. In short, one size does not fit all. But given time and opportunity, top athletes can "do both."

Within this context, then, the remainder of this chapter examines how and why change is currently occurring, what developing dynamics might make further change occur, and how those changes may ultimately lead to more student-athletes attaining a valuable degree. We begin with a discussion of where the power rests within this space through the spectrum of the Sports Power Matrix.

The Sports Power Matrix

Ken introduced the concept of the Sports Power Matrix in his book *Sport Matters: Leadership, Power, and the Quest for Respect in Sports*. Quite simply, the Sports Power Matrix, set forth in Figure 2, is a mechanism through which we can step back and examine the power that exists in sport, and how action, including change, might come about. In *Sport Matters*, the focus of the Sports Power Matrix is on diversity, inclusion, respect, and equality. This framework, however, can similarly be used in the college sports setting to better understand the role of the various parties in bringing about the changes we recommend regarding academic success for student-athletes.

In this college sports version of the Sports Power Matrix, we replace "Ownership" with the "NCAA," "Management" with "Presidents and Conference Commissioners and Athletic Administrators," and "athletes" with "Student-Athletes." The External Stakeholders remain the same.

Student-Athletes

Student-athletes have more power than they may believe, and certainly more than they have leveraged in years past. The temporary nature of their tenure at member institutions is the primary limiting factor on student-athlete activism; their time on campus, ranging from one to maybe five years, is relatively brief compared with the traditional union worker or even professional athletes (with, perhaps, the exception of the NFL). Successes they might achieve in terms of

Figure 2: Sports Power Matrix for College Sports

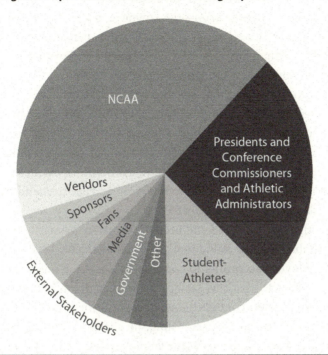

reform may not impact them personally because they are likely to be off campus before the changes are implemented.

Two key events in recent years illustrate the power of student-athletes, past and present. The first is the unionization movement; the second is the ongoing series of lawsuits brought by current and former student-athletes to gain greater rights in several areas.

The Northwestern Unionization Case

In 2014, Peter Sung Ohr, the director of the Chicago district of the National Labor Relations Board, shook the college sport world when he ruled Northwestern University football players could vote to unionize, because they were, in fact, university employees. Though the decision has since been vacated—there will be no union at Northwestern anytime soon—the language in this case presented a compelling argument about the relationship between universities and scholarship athletes. For Ohr, the blatant and obvious prioritization of football over academics was most salient.

At Northwestern, Ohr noted, student-athletes spent as much time working at their sport as a typical full-time employee spends at his or her job. Though football was supposed to be a "supplementary" aspect of their educational experience, the time demands drastically limited their ability to perform in the classroom. For example, scholarship athletes are prohibited from leaving practice to attend class or even taking classes that conflict with it.

As they are recruited and brought to school primarily for their athletic abilities, Ohr found that scholarship athletes are employees. An "employee," according to common-law rules, is someone who, under contract, performs services in exchange for compensation, while the employer controls the services performed and how they are performed.[104] In his 24-page ruling, he characterized the letter of intent and scholarship offer as the employment contract, the revenue and publicity generated as the employer's benefit, the coach's rules as the control, and the scholarship itself as the pay.[105] Though the NCAA and its member institutions denounce this characterization, the perception of exploitation is a growing problem.[106]

Antitrust Lawsuits

Beyond the shifting definition of amateurism, significant antitrust issues played out in at least four major cases. In *Jenkins v. NCAA*, football and basketball players are challenging the lifestyle restrictions the NCAA and its member institutions place on student-athletes. In *Gregory-McGhee v. NCAA*, football players are challenging the disparity between their grants-in-aid and what it actually costs to attend school. Similarly, the plaintiffs in *Alston v. NCAA* argue the limits on grants-in-aid are a result of unlawful collusion between the NCAA and the Big 5 conferences. Finally, the women's basketball players in

Hartman v. NCAA are arguing that the NCAA-imposed limits on their grants-in-aid are a violation of federal antitrust law. These cases share the same underlying fundamental claim: that the NCAA uses the notion of amateurism to restrict the ability of intercollegiate athletes to receive paid services, and thus acts as a cartel.

The NCAA

The power of the NCAA is commonly misunderstood. The NCAA, rather than some monolithic institution, is nothing more than the organization that implements the will of its member institutions. What we need to understand, then, is that it is the member institutions themselves (i.e., the universities), and not NCAA executives such as Mark Emmert, that must make the changes we propose. The NCAA may enforce the rules, but it is the universities themselves that make the rules.

Presidents and Conference Commissioners and Athletics Administrators

Greater clarity is needed regarding the power these individual institutions and conferences have to bring about change.

The primary power in college sport lies with the Power 5 conferences. Reflecting on the possibilities to implement change on the basis of this power, Gordon Gee, the president of West Virginia University and former president of both Ohio State and Vanderbilt, said his experiences at Vanderbilt made clear that "sometimes athletes undervalue academics as part of the academic experience."[107] By totally integrating academics and athletics at Vanderbilt, which was seen as a bold if not risky move at the time, that structure—wherein athletics and academics were elevated to the same importance— helped change the culture. But Gee was clear in noting that such an action can be carried out at only a few American universities. Not every university honestly desires that sort of integration and balance, even taking into account the potential for positive outcomes.

That being said, there seems to be a growing understanding, of sorts, among the Power 5 conferences that reforms are necessary—and perhaps even desirable. As the powerful Pacific-12 Conference commissioner Larry Scott recently reflected, the 65 schools in those five conferences do actually have the ability to be nimbler, to do more, and, yes, to "reform."[108] This new progressive thinking has led to action on such issues as the length of scholarships, the amount of food available for student-athletes, and even concussion protocols. Notably, all of these reforms have been put into action at a pace not seen by member institutions in the past.

Scott made clear that the focus of these universities is not on competitive balance in the tradition of professional teams—the NFL, for instance, prides itself on its system of "parity"—but on competitive balance with regard to resources. And here, of course, is where we see the biggest obstacle to the most significant of reforms. Nobody wants to implement major changes, and perhaps by extension take resources away from winning, unless they know their rivals are doing the same.

Which brings us to perhaps the greatest, and most problematic, "big idea" of reform: that of the demands on athletes' time. Scott himself has noted that there is "more work to do on the time-demands front." In other words, he understands the pressures his players are under; he also understands the mindset of his coaches, who believe that any time you are not spending on the practice field is time that is assisting your competition.

Even taking into account these conflicting interests, there's no question that the power of the Power 5 conferences is real. And in terms of the collegiate Sports Power Matrix, these conferences sit near the top when it comes to the ability to bring about change.

External Stakeholders

It is interesting to note that even in the context of serious reform discussion, there is little concern that fans will move away from following their college teams in the way that there is concern about fans leaving their professional allegiances. Fans' loyalty to their alma mater is much more concrete than their allegiance to any professional team. Thus, that externality is not likely to take much action; they are happy to be along for the ride.

Similarly, sponsors and the media are unlikely to step up on this issue. It would take some kind of massive scandal, or perhaps a series of scandals, or some other disaster for the media to ever reduce the level of coverage or revenues that they send in the direction of college sport.

The government has done its part to step in on occasion, particularly when it comes to finding accurate ways to measure actual graduation rates. Congressional hearings on related topics occur with some frequency, although there is not a great likelihood that change will occur.

Conclusion

The continuing pressure by ever-more-active student-athletes, as well as the rising pressure stemming from lawsuits and the growing independence of the Power 5 conferences, set the stage for dramatic change. As we noted from the outset, most of that change has in years past focused on greater revenue opportunities for student-athletes. As we have also noted throughout, this is fine. The question is, who can lead? The disruption is taking place in a number of forms, but will the revolution be led by the leadership of the NCAA, by college presidents, by powerful conference officials, or by somebody else?

In all reality, the decision to shift our collective attention and resources toward meaningful degree completion does not have to be an either-or proposition. Just as student-athletes have the capability to do both, the system has the capacity to do both as well.

The quote leading into this chapter comes from one of the top athletics directors in the country, Ohio State's Gene Smith. He made these comments at a conference assessing the new state of college sports during the 2017 NCAA Final Four festivities. His statement about the governance structure referenced the nimbleness the Power 5 conferences have now been afforded in getting things done in regard to new policies, student-athlete welfare, and more. The atmosphere for change is only amplified with this renewed era of athlete activism in both unionization and litigation.

Using the Sports Power Matrix as our guide, the players, here the student-athletes, are wielding more power than had ever been anticipated. The idea of success in litigation is not something that had been seen before. Similarly, athlete protest, at the risk of not playing, had largely been absent, too.

Conclusion
Academic and Athletic Success

If the Student-Athlete Manifesto featuring the Meaningful Degree Model were instituted in substantial form and ultimately proved to be successful, where would we be? What difference will we have made? Will we have "fixed" college sports?

Most right-thinking people are likely to conclude that the concept of helping more young people earn meaningful college degrees is a good thing—*just because.* We also set forth earlier the personal benefits that tend to come to those who hold a college degree compared with those who don't.

But why else?

Why make these changes?

Why challenge the system at all?

North Carolina makes clear to us that even when we think we are close to solving the academic issues related to sport at American universities, we are continuing to fall short. The University of North Carolina is one of our greatest public universities. But then the sad story began to unfold; if it can happen at Chapel Hill, can't it happen anywhere?

There are three caveats to remain aware of as you contemplate what could lie ahead if a true refocusing occurs. First, there will always be commentary on how many resources the schools do *not* have— how there are actually only two dozen or so athletic departments, even at the highest level, that are annually profitable.[109] We direct readers, however, to focus not on whether excess funds are available but rather on the idea of reallocating spending that already takes place. Our vision is more about *prioritization* rather than finding ways to spend new revenues.

Second, as we reflected initially, many participating in college sports, and even more rarely at the high school level, will ultimately do fine without college. With that in mind there are some instances where the adage "College is not for everyone" is actually apropos.

Third, there are those, such as the student-athletes featured in the "*30 for 30*" episode about John Calipari aptly titled *One and Not Done*, who are solely focused on becoming professional athletes.[110] They could not be clearer about their aspirations, and as Ohio State's Gene Smith has himself noted, "There are athletes at the top of the pyramid in sports that have no interest in roaming around campus, and that's ok."[111] We agree with them. Without a doubt, then, consideration must be given to the needs of these individuals as well. The bridge that must be built is one that not just allows them to succeed while on campus but invites them back into the educational setting when the time is right *for them*.

Through our proposed reforms, we seek to generate more successes while ensuring that the sadness of Kevin Ross's story never be allowed to occur again. We understand there is no easy solution. But our hope is that the Student-Athlete Manifesto might serve as a roadmap for further discussion to disrupt college sport with this positively impactful reform as the goal.

Acknowledgments

Collin Williams

The acknowledgments cannot begin without first acknowledging the 40 revenue-athletes who participated in my dissertation research. Revenue-athletes are student-athletes who play college sports that generate revenue, namely, Division I men's basketball, football, and sometimes women's basketball. The study juxtaposed the NCAA's espoused goals with these football players' educational and professional expectations and experiences. The sample was composed of 40 seniors from 28 colleges and universities in each of the Power 5 conferences—the Atlantic Coast Conference, the Big Ten Conference, the Big 12 Conference, the Pacific-12 Conference, and the Southeastern Conference. The variety of educational, socioeconomic, and geographic backgrounds from which the participants came is noteworthy. Despite diversity, many commonalities existed among the ways in which they experienced college sports and the amateurism policies governing them. In the spring of 2015 when these football players took the time to inform me about how difficult it was to balance both school and sport, I promised them I would do my best to share their story with the world. Together, we hoped for change.

Important people in their lives, including parents, siblings, friends, and other relatives, introduced revenue-athletes to sports at a young age. The personal relationships formed with other participants (coaches and players) and the success resulting from their physical abilities and commitment to sport led to a love of the game and the development of athletic identities. Many dreamed of playing sports in high school, in college, and professionally. As they grew older and others recognized their athletic prowess and potential, their motivations began to change.

Most frequently, revenue-athletes reported that playing football in college became a means to a financial end. While other motivations included competing at the highest level, continuing a family legacy, enhancing fame and celebrity, and the admiration of family and peers, the vast majority saw playing football in college as an opportunity to help their families, current or future. Many of the 40 seniors viewed an athletic scholarship as a way to lower the cost of college tuition. These were almost exclusively walk-ons and/or white men from middle-class families who had strong academic identities before entering college. According to them, this was not the case for most of their teammates, particularly the scholarship athletes recruited from low-income communities. College, more often than not, was merely a requirement for them to achieve their primary goal: playing professionally and earning a salary to support themselves and their families. For these guys, it was NFL or bust. In fact, without football, many would have forgone college. Still, regardless of background, few felt prepared for the rigors of being a college student and a high-profile athlete.

Shortly after they arrived on campus, revenue-athletes realized that the realities of playing big-time college football are much different from their childhood dreams. They knew they would have to improve their time management skills to balance their academic and athletic responsibilities, but they had no idea how quickly football would be professionalized. While media and recruiting trips tend to glamourize the value of representing your school on game day, coaches typically wait until training camp to make clear exactly how much it takes to earn those opportunities. The extent to which politics influence the allocation of playing time is not explicitly stated but quickly understood. As the revenue generated, coaches' job security and school pride are predicated on winning, players and coaches expectedly prioritize athletic performance over academic success and engagement in other academically purposeful activities or beneficial extracurricular activities. The most pervasive message is sent both overtly and covertly: Football comes first and everything else comes second.

Revenue-athletes' lives are built entirely around football, revenue-athletes are not permitted to schedule classes during practice hours, and they are at all times expected to put forth maximum effort in their athletic endeavors. For those with professional aspirations, there is a rigid five-year window to display their talents on the national stage. Contrarily, there is no set timeline for earning a college degree, spending time with family, preparing for a career after sports, or having a social life. Further, the NFL drafts less than 2% of college athletes, and even fewer secure the lucrative contracts reserved for the elite. Accordingly, as college is the final breeding ground before professional play, Power 5 conference football programs demand athletes, regardless of their personal motivations, spend as much time on their craft as possible. The revenue-athletes estimated they spent at least 40 hours a week on football-related activity—practice, watching film, and competing. These time estimates often exclude study hall, "voluntary" practices, traveling for competition, and resting. Every participant reported his athletic program completely disregarded the 20-hour rule, and little was done to enforce it. The NCAA, they felt, disproportionately focused its energy on punishing student-athletes for accepting extra benefits. Coupled with expectations of always comporting themselves as ambassadors of their respective programs and universities, the time demand placed on revenue-athletes caused them to assert big-time college football is a full-time job for which they are inadequately compensated.

Participation in high-profile college sports affords revenue-athletes opportunities that no other students have, but simultaneously prevents them from engaging in nonathletic activities that make up the "full" college experience. The perceived benefits include athletic scholarships, elite training facilities, and academic and support services, as well as opportunities to travel, represent their universities, and showcase their talents on a national level. There are also the intrinsic values derived from football, like time management, discipline, and the ability to work on a team. No benefit was more frequently cited than the camaraderie and brotherhood formed between the revenue-generating athletes and their teammates. Unfortunately, many of these perceived benefits are directly related to perceived costs. Revenue-athletes reported that the greatest costs of big-time college sports are the arduous schedules resulting from commercialism. As mentioned earlier, athletic scholarships are granted to elite athletes in exchange for the 40+ hours per week spent on football-related activity. With the majority of their time dedicated to perfecting their athletic craft, there is minimal opportunity to engage in academically purposeful activities that result in positive college outcomes—interacting with nonathletic peers and faculty, participating in extracurricular activities, studying abroad, and procuring internships and other professional experiences. Not only do their grades suffer, but so do their critical thinking, social, and professional skills. Bound by their highly structured schedules and engulfed in their athletic roles and communities, revenue-athletes perceive their experiences to be drastically different and frequently separate from those of their peers. Many are not permitted to enroll in certain classes or declare desired majors, and as a result, struggle with decision making after transitioning out of college. Other costs include the risk of injury without comprehensive health insurance and minimal interaction with family. In sum, the athletic prowess that afforded them the opportunity to attend college doesn't allow them enough time to accrue transferable skills and other long-term benefits of a college education.

Additionally, I'd like to acknowledge my dissertation committee, Laura Perna, Scott Rosner, and its chair, Shaun Harper of the USC Race and Equity Center, to whom I am eternally indebted. I am also grateful to every person who has taken the time to read some version of my dissertation or this manuscript and provide feedback. This includes, but is definitely not limited to, Jonathan Berhanu, Kelli Cole, Felecia Commodore, Charles H. F. Davis, Keon McGuire, Demetri Morgan, Cecilia Orphan, Brian Peterson, and Michael Williams.

To Ozzie Newsome, Harry Swayne, Johnny Shelton, and Tricia Bent-Goodley at the Baltimore Ravens; Kathy Behrens, Todd Jacobsen, Greg Taylor, and David Dietz at the NBA; and former Penn men's basketball coach and current Boston Celtics assistant coach Jerome Allen, I thank you for modeling what doing good work with athletes looks like at the college, professional, team, and league levels.

Last but not least, I thank God, family, friends, and fraternity for their unrelenting support. Without my villages of the Psi Chapter of Alpha Phi Alpha, Prep for Prep, Collegiate, Penn, Corona Church, and Antigua, West Indies, none of this would be possible.

Kenneth L. Shropshire

Maybe the older you get the more people you have already acknowledged. I echo Collin's thanks to the athletes. I would also like to acknowledge my wife Diane, my daughter Theresa, and my son Sam, as we have all engaged in sport. With my wife as an All-American and professional tennis player, my daughter having played varsity squash at Stanford, and my son now on the pro tennis circuit after his career at Northwestern, I must also acknowledge I am officially the worst athlete in the family. My four years of practicing "hard" on the Stanford football team and sharing dreams with those other men are always with me. I appreciate all I learned from them and those coaches as well (although they should have let me play!).

Although I did not formally interview anyone at the NCAA for this book, I did seek insight and direction. I also spoke with a number of college sports leaders, as I do on a regular basis. From my personal interactions with many of the leaders, I know the good work they attempt to do in this space. They have a very difficult job.

The same is true with my relationships with player engagement/development specialists across sports. I have spoken with, I am confident, hundreds of these professionals over the years, and as with the NCAA professionals, I look forward to continuing to do so. The job they have begun to take more seriously than ever—athlete degree completion and graduate degree attainment—is something we will hopefully hear much more about going forward. Uniquely in this space, too, I have spent a good deal of time recently with Sean Hobson, the chief design officer at Arizona State University's online division EdPlus. We have spent hours discussing the future of online education, particularly for athletes. I am hopeful that in my next phase in life heading Arizona State's Global Sport Institute we will lead in reform in this area.

One person I have never acknowledged in writing is Professor St. Clair Drake. I have kept a photo of him in my office for decades. He founded the Afro-American Studies program at Stanford, and I had the privilege of taking classes, seminars, and lectures with him and just engaging with him in casual conversations during my undergraduate years. I may have received more academic credits from him than I did from any other professor on Stanford's campus. By far, he opened my eyes the widest. He assigned, along the way, *The Miseducation of the Negro*, by Carter G. Woodson, the book that inspired the title for this work. I thank him for that and for the broader insights that find their way into all of the work that I have done and will continue to do

That was not, however, the first time that I saw that book. My parents were bibliophiles of sorts, and I remember the presence of that book as well as the works of J. A. Rogers (*From Man to Superman*) at a time when the presence of black history written by black historians was virtually nonexistent. The late Jane and Claudius Shropshire find their way into this work via that influence as well.

As always, we acknowledge all of these folks and any good we have delivered is a composite of these various inputs. For sure, as always as well, any mistakes are ours alone. Even as we concluded, Collin, appropriately, began to query all that we had left out and did not cover. Collin and I are optimistic that the conversation we started that led to this book will continue to grow. We look forward to continuing the conversation with you.

Notes

1 C. G. Woodson, *The Mis-education of the Negro* (New York: AMS Press, 1933), 84–85.

2 C. D. Williams, "Student-Athletes' Appraisals of the NCAA Amateurism Policies Governing College Sports" (PhD diss., University of Pennsylvania, 2015), http://repository.upenn.edu/dissertations/AAI3722851.

3 Pseudonym.

4 C. Gaines, "The Highest-Paid Public Employee in 39 US States Is Either a Football or Men's Basketball Coach," Business Insider, September 22, 2016, http://www.businessinsider.com/us-states-highest-paid-public-employee-college-coach-2016-9.

5 D. B. Ridpath, "Financial Incentives for Academic Performance in College Sports Are Never a Good Idea," *Forbes*, November 1, 2016, https://www.forbes.com/sites/bdavidridpath/2016/11/01/financial-incentives-for-academic-performance-in-college-sports-is-never-a-good-idea/#2ab3c16a6eb9.

6 J. Washington, "Big-Time College Athletes Should Be Paid with Big-Time Educations," The Undefeated, April 6, 2017, https://theundefeated.com/features/big-time-college-athletes-should-be-paid-with-big-time-educations/.

7 J. Ma, M. Pender, and M. Welch, *Education Pays 2016: The Benefits of Higher Education for Individuals and Society*, Trends in Higher Education Series, College Board, 2016, https://trends.collegeboard.org/sites/default/files/education-pays-2016-full-report.pdf.

8 C. G. Woodson, *The Mis-education of the Negro* (New York: AMS Press, 1933), 5.

9 Williams, "Student Athletes' Appraisals of the NCAA Amateurism Policies Governing College Sports."

10 R. K. Smith, "A Brief History of the National Collegiate Athletic Association's Role in Regulating Intercollegiate Athletics," *Marquette Sports Law Review* 11, no. 1 (2000): 9–22.

11 Ibid.

12 E. A. Glader, *Amateurism and Athletics* (West Point, NY: Leisure Press, 1978).

13 W. Suggs, *Historical Overview: At Play in America's Colleges. A New Game Plan for College Sport* (Westport, CT: Praeger, 2006).

14 W. Byers and C. Hammer, *Unsportsmanlike Conduct: Exploiting College Athletes* (Ann Arbor: University of Michigan Press, 1995).

15 M. Sperber, *Beer and Circus: How Big-Time College Sports Is Crippling Undergraduate Education* (New York: Henry Holt and Company, 2000).

16 Smith, "A Brief History of the National Collegiate Athletic Association's Role in Regulating Intercollegiate Athletics."

17 Suggs, *Historical Overview.*

18 H. J. Savage, H. W. Bentley, J. T. McGovern, and D. F. Smiley, *American College Athletics* (No. 23), Carnegie Foundation for the Advancement of Teaching, 1929.

19 A. L. Sack and E. J. Staurowsky, *College Athletes for Hire: The Evolution and Legacy of the NCAA's Amateur Myth* (Westport, CT: Praeger, 1998).

20 Suggs, *Historical Overview.*

21 T. Branch, "The Shame of College Sports," *Atlantic Monthly*, October 2011.

22 Byers and Hammer, *Unsportsmanlike Conduct: Exploiting College Athletes.*

23 Branch, "The Shame of College Sports."

24 Suggs, *Historical Overview.*

25 Ibid.

26 Smith, "A Brief History of the National Collegiate Athletic Association's Role in Regulating Intercollegiate Athletics."

27 J. J. Duderstadt, *Intercollegiate Athletics and the American University: A University President's Perspective* (Ann Arbor: University of Michigan Press, 2009).

28 W. Hobson and S. Rich, "Playing in the Red," *Washington Post*, November 23, 2015, http://www.washingtonpost.com/sf/sports/wp/2015/11/23/running-up-the-bills/?utm_term=.159d3006b1f6.

29 M. Tracy, "NCAA Extends Basketball Deal with CBS Sports and Turner through 2032," *New York Times*, April 12, 2016, https://www.nytimes.com/2016/04/13/sports/ncaabasketball/ncaa-extends-basketball-deal-with-cbs-sports-and-turner-through-2032.html.

30 D. Lederman, "The Rule Breakers," Inside Higher Ed, January 11, 2016, https://www.insidehighered.com/news/2016/01/11/96-division-i-colleges-violated-major-ncaa-rules-last-decade.

31 Williams, "Student Athletes' Appraisals of the NCAA Amateurism Policies Governing College Sports."

32 NCAA, "Our Three Divisions," accessed January 20, 2015, http://www.ncaa.org/about/resources/media-center/ncaa-101/our-three-divisions.

33 NCAA, "What Is the NCAA?," accessed January 20, 2015, http://www.ncaa.org/about/resources/media-center/ncaa-101/what-ncaa.

34 NCAA, "The Value of College Sports," accessed January 20, 2015, http://www.ncaa.org/student-athletes/value-college-sports.

35 J. M. Smith and M. Willingham, *Cheated: The UNC Scandal, the Education of Athletes, and the Future of Big-Time College Sports* (Lincoln: University of Nebraska Press, 2015).

36 NCAA, "NCAA Graduation Rates: A Quarter-Century of Tracking Academic Success," October 28, 2014, http://www.ncaa.org/about/resources/research/ncaa-graduation-rates-quarter-century-tracking-academic-success.

37 T. A. Petr and T. S. Paskus, "The Collection and Use of Academic Outcomes Data by the NCAA," *New Directions for Institutional Research, 2009*, no. 144 (2009): 77–92.

38 J. New, "An 'Epidemic' of Academic Fraud," Inside Higher Ed, July 8, 2016, https://www.insidehighered.com/news/2016/07/08/more-dozen-athletic-programs-have-committed-academic-fraud-last-decade-more-likely.

39 NCAA, "NCAA Graduation Rates."

40 NCAA, "Student-Athlete Benefits," accessed January 20, 2015, http://www.ncaa.org/about/resources/finances/student-athlete-benefits.

41 Ibid.

42 NCAA, *Growth, Opportunities, Aspirations and Learning of Students in College (GOALS) Study*, 2015, http://www.ncaa.org/about/resources/research/ncaa-goals-study.

43 *Understanding Life Outcomes of Former NCAA Student-Athletes: The Gallup-Purdue Index Report*, 2016, http://www.ncaa.org/about/resources/research/gallup-study-life-outcomes-former-student-athletes.

44 Ibid.

45 New, "An 'Epidemic' of Academic Fraud."

46 S. R. Harper, C. D. Williams, and H. W. Blackman, *Black Male Student-Athletes and Racial Inequities in NCAA Division I College Sports* (Philadelphia: University of Pennsylvania, Center for the Study of Race and Equity in Education, 2013).

47 NCAA, "NCAA Graduation Rates."

48 NCAA, *Growth, Opportunities, Aspirations and Learning of Students in College (GOALS) Study.*

49 J. G. Gaston-Gayles, "Engaging Student Athletes," in *Student Engagement in Higher Education: Theoretical Perspectives and Practical Approaches for Diverse Populations*, ed. S. R. Harper and S. J. Quaye (New York: Routledge, 2015), 209–20.

50 S. K. Watt and J. L. Moore, "Who Are Student Athletes?," in *Student Services for Athletes*, ed. M. F. Howard-Hamilton and S. K. Watt, New Directions for Student Services, no. 93 (San Francisco: Jossey-Bass, 2001), 7–18.

51 B. Wolverton, "Athletes' Hours Renew Debate over College Sports," *Chronicle of Higher Education* 54, no. 20, January 25, 2008, http://www.chronicle.com/article/Athletes-Hours-Renew-Debate/22003.

52   J. R. Potuto and J. O'Hanlon, "National Study of Student Athletes Regarding Their Experiences as College Students," 2006, accessed May 31, 2011, http://www.ncaa.org/library/research/studentathlete_experiences/2006/2006_sa_experience.pdf.

53   P. Adler and P. A. Adler, "Role Conflict and Identity Salience: College Athletics and the Academic Role," *Social Science Journal* 24, no. 4 (1987): 443–55.

54   P. A. Adler and P. Adler, "The Gloried Self: The Aggrandizement and the Constriction of Self," *Social Psychology Quarterly* 52, no. 4 (1989): 299–310.

55   P. Adler and P. A. Adler, *Backboards & Blackboards: College Athletics and Role Engulfment* (New York: Columbia University Press, 1991).

56   K. K. Beamon, " 'I'm a Baller': Athletic Identity Foreclosure among African-American Former Student-Athletes," *Journal of African American Studies* 16, no. 2 (2012): 195–208.

57   M. F. Howard-Hamilton and S. K. Watt, *Student Services for Athletes*, New Directions for Student Services, no. 93 (San Francisco: Jossey-Bass, 2001).

58   C. M. Engstrom and W. E. Sedlacek, "A Study of Prejudice toward University Student-Athletes," *Journal of Counseling & Development* 70, no. 1 (1991): 189–93.

59   E. Comeaux and C. K. Harrison, "Faculty and Male Student Athletes: Racial Differences in the Environmental Predictors of Academic Achievement," *Race, Ethnicity and Education* 10, no. 2 (2007): 199–214.

60   J. Coakley, *Sport in Society: Issues & Controversies*, 10th ed. (Boston: McGraw-Hill, 2009).

61   J. McKenna and H. Thomas, "Enduring Injustice: A Case Study of Retirement from Professional Rugby Union," *Sport, Education and Society* 12, no. 1 (2007): 19–35.

62   S. Park, D. Lavallee, and D. Tod, "Athletes' Career Transition out of Sport: A Systematic Review," *International Review of Sport and Exercise Psychology* 6, no. 1 (2013): 22–53.

63   F. M. Perna, R. L. Ahlgren, and L. Zaichkowsky, "The Influence of Career Planning, Race, and Athletic Injury on Life Satisfaction among Recently Retired Collegiate Male Athletes," *Sport Psychologist* 13 (1999): 144–56.

64   P. Lally, "Identity and Athletic Retirement: A Prospective Study," *Psychology of Sport and Exercise* 8, no. 1 (2007): 85–99.

65   K. Warriner and D. Lavallee, "The Retirement Experiences of Elite Female Gymnasts: Self Identity and the Physical Self," *Journal of Applied Sport Psychology* 20, no. 3 (2008): 301–17.

66   Williams, "Student Athletes' Appraisals of the NCAA Amateurism Policies Governing College Sports."

67   B. Strauss, "Northwestern Quarterback Makes His Case for Players' Union," *New York Times*, February 18, 2014, https://www.nytimes.com/2014/02/19/sports/ncaafootball/northwestern-quarterback-makes-his-case-for-players-union.html?mcubz=0&_r=0.

68   J. Torry, "Does Ohio State's President Favor Paying College Athletes?," *Columbus Dispatch*, April 26, 2017, http://www.dispatch.com/news/20170426/does-ohio-states-president-favor-paying-college-athletes.

69   Ibid.

70   Smith, "A Brief History of the National Collegiate Athletic Association's Role in Regulating Intercollegiate Athletics."

71   Savage, Bentley, McGovern, and Smiley, *American College Athletics*.

72   Sperber, *Beer and Circus*.

73   Smith, "A Brief History of the National Collegiate Athletic Association's Role in Regulating Intercollegiate Athletics."

74   "After Fleeing from War-Torn Sudan, Dau Jok Becomes a Leader at Penn," *Sports Illustrated*, January 23, 2013, http://www.si.com/basketball/2013/01/23/dau-jok-penn.

75   Sperber, *Beer and Circus*.

76   J. R. Thelin, *Games Colleges Play: Scandal and Reform in Intercollegiate Athletics* (Baltimore: Johns Hopkins University Press, 2011).

77   Harper, Williams, and Blackman, *Black Male Student-Athletes and Racial Inequities in NCAA Division I College Sports*.

78   Ma, Pender, and Welch, *Education Pays 2016*.

79   W. Berry, "Amending Amateurism: Saving Intercollegiate Athletics through Conference-Athlete Revenue Sharing," *Alabama Law Review* 68, no. 2 (2016): 551–81.

80   Ma, Pender, and Welch, *Education Pays 2016*.

81   Williams, "Student Athletes' Appraisals of the NCAA Amateurism Policies Governing College Sports."

82   S. R. Harper and J. K. Donnor, eds. *Scandals in College Sports* (New York: Routledge, 2017).

83   T. Waldron, "UNC Is the Perfect NCAA Champion, and Not in a Good Way," *Huffington Post*, April 4, 2017, http://www.huffingtonpost.com/entry/ncaa-basketball-north-carolina-student-athletes-scandal_us_58e2ac18e4b03a26a3652cf6.

84   NCAA, "The First in Their Family," accessed February 7, 2017, http://www.ncaa.org/about/resources/research/first-their-family.

85 J. Curry, "Suing for Second Chance to Start Over," *New York Times,* January 30, 1990, http://www.nytimes.com/1990/01/30/sports/suing-for-2d-chance-to-start-over.html?pagewanted=all&mcubz=0.

86 Prep for Prep, http://www.prepforprep.org.

87 E. P. St. John, S. Hu, and A. S. Fisher, *Breaking Through the Access Barrier: How Academic Capital Formation Can Improve Policy in Higher Education* (New York: Routledge, 2010).

88 S. R. Harper, C. D. Williams, D. Pérez II, and D. L. Morgan, "His Experience: Toward a Phenomenological Understanding of Academic Capital Formation among Black and Latino Male Students," in *Readings on Equal Education 26,* ed. R. Winkle-Wagner, P. J. Bowman, and E. P. St. John (New York: AMS Press, 2012).

89 Williams, "Student Athletes' Appraisals of the NCAA Amateurism Policies Governing College Sports."

90 J. Tipton, "UK's 'Lifetime Scholarship' Turns Oliver White's 'Nightmare' into Dream Come True," KentuckySports, April 29, 2017, http://www.kentucky.com/sports/college/kentucky-sports/uk-basketball-men/article147610794.html.

91 C. Patterson, "Maryland to Offer Lifetime Scholarships for All Athletes," CBS Sports, August 19, 2014, http://www.cbssports.com/college-football/news/maryland-to-offer-lifetime-scholarships-for-all-athletes/.

92 Williams, "Student Athletes' Appraisals of the NCAA Amateurism Policies Governing College Sports."

93 S. Berger, "Full-Time College Athletes Should Be Part-Time Students," *Sports Illustrated,* January 12, 2017, https://www.si.com/college-basketball/2017/01/12/ncaa-student-athletes-scholarships-basketball-football.

94 Williams, "Student Athletes' Appraisals of the NCAA Amateurism Policies Governing College Sports."

95 NCAA, Article 17 of the *2014–2015 NCAA DI Manual,* 2014, 223.

96 Ibid.

97 Williams, "Student Athletes' Appraisals of the NCAA Amateurism Policies Governing College Sports."

98 "Independence & History," accessed February 24, 2017, https://www.usada.org/about/independence-history/.

99 S. R. Harper, *Black Male Student-Athletes and Racial Inequities in NCAA Division I College Sports* (Philadelphia: University of Pennsylvania, Center for the Study of Race and Equity in Education, 2016).

100 Harper, Williams, and Blackman, *Black Male Student-Athletes and Racial Inequities in NCAA Division I College Sports.*

101 Comments by Gene Smith, SLB Conference, "Spring 2017: Sport Law and Business Final Four Symposium: Full Court Press: Media, Autonomy, and the Future of

College Sports" (Sandra Day O'Connor School of Law, Phoenix, Arizona, April 3, 2017).

102 P. Watley, "Cops Subdue Ex-basketball Player Kevin Ross in Hotel Rampage," *Chicago Tribune*, July 24, 1987, http://articles.chicagotribune.com/1987-07-24/news/8702240109_1_basketball-player-kevin-ross-squad-cars-james-maurer.

103 ESPN, "Outside the Lines: Unable to Read," ESPN.com, March 17, 2002, http://www.espn.com/page2/tvlistings/show103transcript.html.

104 P. Vint, "Explaining What the Northwestern College Football Union Decision Means," SBNation.com, March 27, 2014, http://www.sbnation.com/collegefootball/2014/3/27/5551014/college-football-players-union-northwestern-nlrb.

105 Ibid.

106 W. Berry, "Amending Amateurism."

107 Comments by Gordon Gee, SLB Conference, "Spring 2017: Sport Law and Business Final Four Symposium: Full Court Press: Media, Autonomy, and the Future of College Sports" (Sandra Day O'Connor School of Law, Phoenix, Arizona, April 3, 2017).

108 Comments by Larry Scott, SLB Conference, "Spring 2017: Sport Law and Business Final Four Symposium: Full Court Press: Media, Autonomy, and the Future of College Sports" (Sandra Day O'Connor School of Law, Phoenix, Arizona, April 3, 2017).

109 B. Burnsed, "Athletics Departments That Make More Than They Spend Still a Minority," NCAA.org, September 18, 2015, http://www.ncaa.org/about/resources/media-center/news/athletics-departments-make-more-they-spend-still-minority.

110 J. Hock, "ESPN 30 for 30: One and Not Done," ESPN.com, accessed May 6, 2017, http://www.espn.com/30for30/film?page=OneAndNotDone.

111 Comments by Gene Smith, SLB Conference.

Index

Note: Page numbers in italics refer to figures or tables.

About the Authors

Kenneth L. Shropshire

Kenneth L. Shropshire is the CEO of the Global Sport Institute and the adidas Distinguished Professor of Global Sport at Arizona State University. He recently closed out a 30-year career as an endowed full professor at the Wharton School of the University of Pennsylvania, where he was also director of the Wharton Sports Business Initiative, professor of Africana studies, and academic director of Wharton's sports-focused executive education programs. He now holds the title of Wharton Endowed Professor Emeritus.

His career has been highlighted by leading the launch of several noteworthy ventures in a variety of sectors, including leading the boxing competition during the last profitable Olympic Games, which was also the most televised event of the games in 1984; founding and leading the Wharton Sports Business Initiative, one of the world's most respected sports business think tanks, in 2004; serving as a founder and board member of the Valley Green Bank, which was sold to Univest Corp. for $76 million in 2014; and guiding the launch of the nonprofit Ross Initiative in Sports for Equality (RISE) in 2016 and serving on its board. As a sports industry leader, he is former president of the Sports Lawyers Association, the largest such organization in the world, and also former program chair of the ABA Forum Committee, Sports Law Section. His views and insights on the sports industry can be heard weekly on SiriusXM's Wharton Sports Business Show, which he cohosts.

He has written several books, including the recent titles *Sport Matters: Leadership, Power, and the Quest for Respect in Sports*;

Negotiate Like the Pros: A Top Sports Negotiator's Lessons for Making Deals, Building Relationships and Getting What You Want; and *Being Sugar Ray: The Life of America's Greatest Boxer and First Celebrity Athlete*. Additional works include the foundational books *In Black and White: Race and Sports in America*; *The Business of Sports;* and *The Business of Sports Agents.*

Shropshire's consulting roles have featured a wide variety of projects, including work for the NCAA, Major League Baseball, National Football League, National Football League Players Association, the United States Olympic Committee, and PGA (Professional Golf Association) golfer Rory McIlroy. In addition to RISE, he serves on the board of directors of Moelis & Company (a global independent investment bank) and on the nonprofit board of USA Volleyball, and serves as an adviser to the Sixers Innovation Lab.

Shropshire earned an undergraduate degree in economics from Stanford University and a law degree from Columbia University, and is a member of the California bar. He joined the law firm of Manatt, Phelps, Rothenberg and Tunney in Los Angeles prior to working with the 1984 Olympic Games and beginning his lengthy career at Wharton.

Collin D. Williams, Jr.

Collin D. Williams, Jr., is an educator, author, and researcher addressing issues of race, gender, and socioeconomic status through the lens of sport. He is currently the director of leadership and education programs in the South region for the Ross Initiative in Sports for Equality (RISE).

Previously, he worked in Social Responsibility and Player Programs for the National Basketball Association, providing comprehensive support for the Leadership Together program, using the NBA brand to bring together youth, parents, law enforcement, and community leaders to dialogue about race, implicit bias, and policing.

As the assistant director of Player Engagement for the Baltimore Ravens of the National Football League, Collin assisted players with their transitions into, through, and out of the NFL. Using programming and mentoring, he offered strategies to connect their current and future needs with relevant and timely National Football League Players Association resources, from player assistance services to second career training opportunities and continuing education advising. Focused on education, he helped design and execute the Rookie Symposium, Orientation, and Success Program.

During his tenure as a doctoral student of higher education at the University of Pennsylvania's Graduate School of Education, Collin served as a research associate and campus climate consultant at the Center for the Study of Race & Equity in Education, as a residential associate in College Houses and Academic Services, and as an instructor of a graduate-level interactive seminar course on issues of US diversity.

His research explores how undergraduates' social experiences influence engagement, academic performance, campus climate, and postcollege outcomes, especially for students and athletes of color from low-income, first-generation college, and other underrepresented backgrounds. *Sports Illustrated, ESPN, Huffington Post, the Washington Post, TIME* magazine, and over 300 other national and local media outlets have featured and quoted his work.

About Wharton School Press

Wharton School Press, the book publishing arm of The Wharton School of the University of Pennsylvania, was established to inspire bold, insightful thinking within the global business community.

Wharton School Press publishes a select list of award-winning, bestselling, and thought-leading books that offer trusted business knowledge to help leaders at all levels meet the challenges of today and the opportunities of tomorrow. Led by a spirit of innovation and experimentation, Wharton School Press leverages groundbreaking digital technologies and has pioneered a fast-reading business book format that fits readers' busy lives, allowing them to swiftly emerge with the tools and information needed to make an impact. Wharton School Press books offer guidance and inspiration on a variety of topics, including leadership, management, strategy, innovation, entrepreneurship, finance, marketing, social impact, public policy, and more.

Wharton School Press also operates an online bookstore featuring a curated selection of influential books by Wharton School faculty and Press authors published by a wide range of leading publishers.

To find books that will inspire and empower you to increase your impact and expand your personal and professional horizons, visit *wsp.wharton.upenn.edu.*

About The Wharton School

Founded in 1881 as the world's first collegiate business school, the Wharton School of the University of Pennsylvania is shaping the future of business by incubating ideas, driving insights, and creating leaders who change the world. With a faculty of more than 235 renowned professors, Wharton has 5,000 undergraduate, MBA, Executive MBA, and doctoral students. Each year 18,000 professionals from around the world advance their careers through Wharton Executive Education's individual, company-customized, and online programs. More than 99,000 Wharton alumni form a powerful global network of leaders who transform business every day.

For more information, visit *www.wharton.upenn.edu.*